P9-BZD-676

RING A DOZEN DOORBELLS

By
Helen Good Brenneman

Photographs by David Hiebert

Twelve
Women Tell It
Like It Is

HERALD PRESS Scottdale, Pa. 15683

1973

Library of Congress Cataloging in Publication Data

Brenneman, Helen Good.
   Ring a dozen doorbells.

   1. Women in the United States — Biography. I. Title.
CT3260.B77   920.72'0973   72-6601
ISBN 0-8361-1702-6

RING A DOZEN DOORBELLS
Copyright © 1973 by Herald Press, Scottdale, Pa. 15683
Library of Congress Catalog Card Number: 72-6601
International Standard Book Number: 0-8361-1702-6
Printed in the United States
Designed by Alice B. Shetler

To My Liberated Friends

Preface

In my recent book, *The House by the Side of the Road,* I made the statement, "There is no stereotype of homemaker image into which every American woman must fit. The exciting thing about being a homemaker is that each woman can create her own special variety of wifehood and motherhood, according to her interests, abilitites, and personality. . . . We will each bring beauty and comfort to the lives of our families in our own way, with our own specialties, hobbies, insights, and aptitudes. . . . There just isn't any law to prescribe how we American women must go about being wives and mothers."

In the chapter, "Lucky Girl," I described some of my friends who live creatively and with imagination and purpose. The more I thought about these friends, each dwelling under her own vine and fig tree in her own way, the more I wanted to listen to their stories, to find out more about their motivations, insights, circumstances, and philosophies. However, it would have been easier to choose the friends about whom I would write, if I had set out to write a book entitled *Ring Six Dozen Doorbells.* I am ever astounded by the wealth of friendships God has granted me.

So will you come along, as I make the rounds to twelve of my friends, ringing their doorbells and sitting down with them over a cup of tea? We can be grateful to these women, who were willing to share their innermost thoughts, struggles, failures, successes, hopes, and dreams. They talked freely and with candor. No one will agree with everything that each of our friends has to say. But my hope is that as you read these stories of living women of our time, you will identify with some of them, sorting through their ideas and picking up some helpful concepts which will be workable for you.

My purpose in writing this book is to try to show from the examples of these twelve outstanding women that there are as many ways of being a woman as there are varieties of individuals. And in a day when models in marriage are undergoing change and there is much discussion on the role of women, marriage responsibilities can be restructured in a variety of ways. The only caution is that the arrangement be mutually acceptable to *both* parties, that there is a *conjoint* plan for the lives of the couple, and that no real babies are thrown out with any bath water. I have also included chapters, however, about single and widowed friends, as all of us know many women who are making invaluable contributions without marriage partners.

It may appear that I am partial to certain names, such as Doris and Ruth, but the predominance of these names is coincidental. I chose my interviewees for what they had to say.

One reaction which was common to most of my friends when they had read their stories, was that perhaps I had treated them too well. They wanted it made clear that although they had high ideals, they had their bad days and sometimes fell short of their aims and purposes.

Another problem with writing a book about living people is that between the time of the initial interview and the final publication date some circumstances will change, children become older, and with experience and more maturity we may adjust some of our own ideas about things. However, I do not believe that basic values will be altered with the passing of time.

In addition to those women about whom I have written and who willingly gave us a glimpse into their everyday lives, I want to thank my husband, Virgil, who accompanied me as I rang some of the doorbells, and my young friend, journalism student, photographer David Hiebert, who good-naturedly hitchhiked his way around the country, following my interviews with his camera. In the closing stages of manuscript preparation I was also surrounded by a group of caring friends who read sections of the book and offered helpful suggestions. Of these I would like to particularly mention Mrs. Harold S. Bender, who helped in putting the finishing touches on the book.

Contents

Doris Schrock: I'm excited with my teenagers. I'm not as worried about youth as about older people.

Homemaker Plus

When Virgil and I rang Doris and Allen Schrock's doorbell, we entered a higher story than in bygone years when we frequented their basement home. And in a way, it symbolized their life as a couple, for we had had the joy of knowing them on the ground floor of their family life and now watched them enter a new chapter, living with a houseful of teenagers.

"How do you like being middle-aged?" I asked Doris, as the four of us seated ourselves in the newly completed living room with its picture window overlooking, beyond their wooded, two-acre lot, Indiana's rolling countryside as far as eye could see.

"I love it," was her characteristically enthusiastic response. "I have a whole circle of young friends right here in my own house. And I find them tremendously exciting. The kids say I'm prejudiced. Ruthie says, 'Mother, you have too high an opinion of us. You make us think too much of ourselves.' "

School principal Allen rejoined, "I think this is a good thing, because kids tend to live up to your expectations. They have a goal to shoot for."

As we talked, I remembered Doris in the houseful-of-little-children stage of her life. The basement house was a real advantage, so far as the children were concerned. There was plenty of time to live together as a family, and it was not necessary to fuss over the house. The Schrocks knew that eventually they would build upward on their redwood two-story frame house, but they planned to do it as time and money made the building possible. In the meantime, they were anything but tense about it. The five children, who were born 1-2-3-4-5 in six years, enjoyed an enriched life with parents who had prayed for their coming and thanked God for their presence.

I remembered those basement years in the life of the Schrocks with affection, as it was during that time that we were members of the same congregation and spent much time talking over ideas while our children, similar in age and sex, played together and built their own friendships.

"Our children never had kindergarten," Doris recalled, "but I don't think they suffered, because we had kindergarten at home. Having a teacher for a father was a plus for the children because Allen just filled our home with pictures and words and ideas that kept the children excited intellectually. We did a lot of cutting and coloring, made jigsaw puzzles out of plywood, and built things with Tinker Toys. The children were always learning something, the alphabet or their numbers. We would give them little things to do, such as to bring *two* forks and *three* spoons."

Allen told of making two sets of bunk beds, a triple-decker for Ruth, Naomi, and Paul, and a double-decker for Joe and Dave. And we all remembered the swings hanging from the rafters of the basement living room, a phenomenon which might never have occurred if they had been living in the finished house. The outside was an additional source of pleasure, with the acres of lawn, a pond, and plenty of trees for climbing. "The children still talk about the good times we had those days," Doris said. "We'd pack a lunch at noon and walk all the way to the back of the lot, taking Kool-Aid in catsup bottles as our 'pop.'"

"What I remember," I mentioned, "was the neat way you had of putting the children's things away."

"Yes," Doris said, "Every child had his own drawer in a chest, and a box for his belongings. And we usually put things away together, making a game of seeing who could pick up the most. I know the children appreciated having a place to put their things, because one of the first questions they asked about heaven was whether they could take their drawer along. Since I was sure they would have anything they needed, I assured them that they could. After they were older, the subject came up again and we realized with some amusement how our concepts of heaven change as we mature."

The five children, who arrived early in the marriage of Doris and Allen, were neither a surprise nor an intrusion. Actually, their love of children had been a topic of conversation on their very first date, incidentally, to be sure, when they had passed children on the highway and Doris had remarked that she liked children and admired large families. Not until later in their courtship did she learn why Allen had thrown back his head with a hearty laugh. It seems that he had had the same thought.

The very fact that Doris and Allen met at all was an act of Providence, for although they were both brought up in rural Illinois communities, their paths might never have crossed except for a strange coincidence.

Allen, a student at what is now Western Illinois University in Malcolm, had stayed in town for the weekend in order to attend a special function. Somehow this program did not materialize, and Allen found himself driving around town on Saturday evening, wondering how he would spend his weekend. Suddenly he noticed a little white frame church, all lighted up and with cars parked in front. Although he was wearing a T-shirt and suntans (similar to modern jeans), he decided to see what was going on inside.

What was happening in that small Free Methodist Church was that Doris, a youth evangelist, was conducting a special service. She noticed the young man come in and was encouraged when he returned on Sunday morning and again on other evenings of her youth emphasis week, bringing other college students with him. That first Sunday, after they shared in a Sunday school class discussion, Allen offered to take her for a ride to see the surrounding countryside, since she was a visitor in the community.

"Was there a special aura when you were together?" Virgil joked, as Doris and Allen repeated the story of their meeting.

Doris laughed. "There seemed to be a cloud over Allen, with lightning coming out of it," she told us. "One morning we were in prayer at the church, and I felt him coming before he got into the building. But the thing which really impressed me was that on our first date he asked if we could have prayer together before we said good night. I had never heard of such a thing, and he scored a lot of points that night. We continued this practice throughout our courtship."

From the time that Allen and Doris met, from June of 1949 until they were married the following June, they never missed a day in writing to one another. Allen continued his senior year of college, graduating shortly before their wedding, and Doris, who had already received a degree in philosophy and religion, continued youth work in her church, traveling a circuit to various congregations and commuting periodically to her home. To make a short story even shorter — in spite of all this activity, the couple were able to get together about once a month and became acquainted with one another's families.

But Doris, trained for a life vocation in church work, and prepared to teach Bible in college, had to be certain that this new development in her life was not wishful thinking, but was indeed the will of God. Some acquaintances did not help matters much.

"I was told by older people, who like to mold your life for you, that I was marked for single blessedness, and for years of giving myself to the church. I am not good at making my own decisions, and I like to be told what to do, but I didn't like what they were telling me. One man said that I would be frustrated all my life, that whenever I heard someone else speak, I would think that I could have done it better. But I have never felt that way.

"It called for a lot of prayer," Doris summarized. "But the Lord made His will known in a number of specific ways, and I was really at peace when we were married. And I have found lots of ways to serve God since then."

Taking their honeymoon to North Carolina, the Schrocks made arrangements for Allen to enter graduate school at the University of North Carolina in August. Living frugally on his income provided by the GI Bill of Rights, they rented a trailer, to which Allen added an extra room. They bought a refrigerator for $25, made a desk out of scrap lumber and cardboard boxes, picked nuts in the nearby woods, and canned produce given them by friends in a local church. While Allen was working on his master's degree in physical education and health, Doris, an avid reader, enjoyed a brief respite and began transforming ten yards of flannel into a layette for their first child.

Then, after a brief sojourn in Illinois, the Schrocks built their basement house near Goshen, Indiana, and began the chapter which Doris describes as "the happiest years of my life."

"I remember you had so many interests then, Doris," I brought up. "Your Bible memorization, for instance."

"Yes, I did feel the need to keep improving myself,

spiritually and in every other way. I tried to learn French from records, and there was that challenge to memorize Scripture."

Doris explained how that all started: she heard a minister quote Martin Luther that the Book of Romans should be committed to memory. This minister knew of only one man who had done so.

"I suppose it would take the rest of my life, but I thought it was something I could do. It went very well, and I had the book memorized in just a few weeks. It was so exciting and such a blessing, that I was challenged to go on."

I could see Doris those days in my mind's eye, for I remembered how she had cut up a Testament and posted it above her kitchen sink, how she mowed their enormous lawn with pages from a Testament under her one hand, how she gardened with her Testament, how she memorized while ironing. And she did not stop until she had memorized all the New Testament except the four Gospels, the Book of Revelation, and the last part of 2 Corinthians.

"Did the children resent your memorizing?" I asked.

"I would talk aloud, though softly, and they would hear me and say, 'Oh, Mommy's memorizing.' But they knew they could interrupt, I never cut them off when they wanted to talk. I never did it when the children needed me. I never broke into our story time, and I always lay down with them when they had their naps. It never pays to be rude to children.

"It was a good spiritual and mental exercise," she went on, "and certain Scriptures opened to me in a way they never had before."

I recalled services at which Doris had repeated whole chapters of the New Testament, and she felt that she could still do so, if she had a bit of warning so that she could brush up on a passage.

During the early years of their family life a new vista opened for Doris. It all began one night when she was tucking the children in bed and the thought came to her, what would she do if something happened to Allen? When she voiced this feeling to her husband, he asked, "Would you like to go back to school and get a teacher's certificate?"

Allen knew that Doris loved school, and that it would not take her long to qualify as a teacher. "To me, this spelled security," Doris remembers. "I didn't think of it as being as useful as it has been."

The Schrocks had long before begun a life-style which made Doris' evening classes (one each semester) a possibility without imposing a hardship on the children. Each morning everyone arose early and the children were dressed so that before Allen went to work the family could sit down to the breakfast table together for morning worship. Then in the evening, after a satisfying story hour, the children went to bed willingly no later than 7:00 or 7:30. Doris usually read to the children and Allen listened, and they kept this custom faithfully until Joe was fifteen years old. When the children had to catch a 7:00 a.m. school bus, their habit of early to bed and early rising was a real bonanza.

Doris did not begin actual teaching until all her children were in school. Up to that time she took all her classes in the evening except the year she did her student teaching. Since there was no kindergarten in her area that year, Naomi sometimes accompanied her to the library, sitting under the table and playing with Doris' shoes while she studied, or enjoyed an afternoon with a neighbor who had a little girl her own age.

Doris' appetite for elementary teaching was whetted by living with a teaching enthusiast, helping him with grading standardized tests or typing, and entertaining his students and fellow-teachers. Teaching was also appealing because of the hours. By teaching in her own area, Doris was able to go to school when her children left in the morning, and return home at the same time in the afternoon.

"How have you managed to get your work done at home since you have been teaching?" I asked Doris, since I knew that working couples have various ways of dividing up the household chores.

Again Doris emphasized how their early morning hours were an advantage.

"Before I go to school I'm usually able to do the routine housework and plan my evening meal so that I can prepare a dessert, for instance, while I am washing the breakfast dishes. Allen leaves very early because he teaches in South Bend, and the children take care of their own rooms. Then I usually start the laundry as soon as I get home, and after supper I do some special project such as mending or ironing, something each day."

"Does Allen help around the house, other than his outside work and construction on the house?"

Allen said that in earlier years he had sometimes

taken the wash to the laundromat and had done a great deal of grocery shopping. But Doris hastened to explain how she felt on the subject.

"I don't go along with these modern young people on TV, who think their husbands don't love them if they don't help with the dishes, carry out the garbage, or bring them breakfast in bed. I never thought this was a man's place. In my home Mom had her role and Dad had his, and I never saw them cross over unless there was illness. My father was a rural mail carrier, and although there was a substitute carrier for sickness, Mom often had to do some of it. And Dad could work in the kitchen. When Mother was ill, he taught me how to cook. But these were emergencies."

Virgil brought up the fact that Doris' mother did not work outside the home.

"Sometimes I'm tempted to think about that," Doris said. "But I think I'm unusually healthy and everything is so convenient for me that I can handle two jobs quite well. With the house, the cars, and the grounds, there is so much other work for Allen to do. This way of sharing works out well for us."

"And how about the kids? How do they help out?"

Doris admitted that she did not consider herself very good at training children to work, but that they had somehow learned in spite of this.

"My children never were assigned regular chores. So-and-so does the dishes on such-and-such-a-night, or this one has to do this and another one that," she said. "We've always just done what needed to be done, and more often someone has volunteered to work." She mentioned that her older daughter could easily go into the kitchen and do a complete meal. She also frequently took care of the laundry.

"I firmly believe that any girl can learn to do anything she needs to learn in just a few days if she has to," she went on. Then she told of her own experience in earning money for college. She had informed her employer that she couldn't iron white shirts, to which the lady responded, "You can't or you won't?" She got the message and ironed white shirts!

I had always been fascinated by the story of the summer that the Schrocks got along without their mother. It was after Doris had been teaching for a few years, that she decided to concentrate a summer at Indiana University, gaining nine hours toward her master's degree, and following later with night courses at a university extension closer home.

"How did it go?" I asked Allen, who assured me that so far as he could remember, everything went fine. By that time Joe was 14 and Ruthie 12, and they proudly took over the meal planning, shopping, and cooking.

"They used more convenience foods, and since they read well, they had no trouble following the instructions on the box," Doris told us, then added that there had been only one minor casualty during that summer. One of her sons had never thought to launder his sheet during the entire six-week period! "I still have one tan sheet," she laughed, "but when I got home, it took only a few days to get things back into shape."

The summer that Doris was away at school gave the family another idea and inspired one of their happiest summer experiences the following year. Everyone went to school that summer. Motoring to Bloomington, Indiana, the Schrocks, veteran campers, set up camp in a state park for a week until they were able to move into a rented, furnished house. Then Allen worked on his principal's license, Doris completed her degree, Joe took driver's training for credit, Dave took a credited science course with a reservoir project, Ruthie studied art and mathematics, and Paul and Naomi took enrichment courses in an experimental school. Besides their studies, the entire family had a membership at a swimming pool, the boys learned to play tennis, and the children, accustomed to living in the country, had the pleasure of walking downtown. It was hot that summer, but no one complained.

One of the best learning projects of the Schrock family has been the gradual construction of their home, which grew as the children grew and to which all of them could contribute. In 1960 Allen hired a carpenter crew to frame in the upper stories of the house and he took time to paint it, even though that was the summer of their big camping trip to the West Coast. The second story was completed first, so that the children could begin sleeping there. Then the children got into the act, pounding nails, cutting tar paper off the floor, putting on the ceiling of the main floor, and painting their rooms. Although the house is now completed, there are still details to be done, as most homeowners can understand.

But Doris, thinking over these parent-child projects, considers them priceless in passing on values.

"I think example is more important than anything we say," she commented. "As I watch the boys growing up, I see in each of them different things that I know they've imbibed from Allen. He never told them these things, but they just picked them up from working with him, being with him, and seeing the way he does things. And I think the girls get things from me, too."

She went on to tell an experience which had happened very recently. She had commended Ruthie on the way she had cleaned up the kitchen, and Ruthie had responded, "Where do you think I learned it?" It was Doris' turn to feel complimented.

"Of course," Doris admitted, "if she sees things in me that she doesn't like, she doesn't practice these. But I believe that we need to make attractive those things which we think are important. Some people hate to do dishes because they know their mother always hated to do them."

"Even though we don't get together often these days, Doris," I said, "I've noticed in telephone conversations with you that you aren't pushing the panic button about today's young people."

Doris smiled. "I'm not so worried about the youth as I am about the older people."

"Meaning what?"

"I'm afraid they're going to make it so hard for our young people, whom I see as wonderful and beautiful. When I lived on the farm, I saw a horse having to be held so tightly that he "busted a hame," and had to be destroyed. From the farmer's point of view, he had to hold back that horse, but you can't do this with young people. You have to guide them with words and caresses, not with pitchforks and whips. Yes, you have to keep a hand on the reins, but it has to be a loose one."

We paused to discuss the Schrock children briefly, Joe, 20 and a psychology major who would be a college junior the next year; Dave, 19 and a sophomore interested in sociology; Ruthie, 18 and just ready for college; and the two high school students, Paul, 17, and Naomi, 15.

We talked about their musical interests, the singing groups to which they belonged and the instruments they played. We talked about their special aptitudes, two of the boys for drama, Ruthie's creative activities and participation in the Presidential Classroom for Young Americans in Washington, their enthusiasms and their hopes. But most important, each had come individually to parents or pastor to announce his decision to accept Christ and become a member of the church. Now they helped, along with their parents, in the work of a small, racially integrated congregation in South Bend.

"One thing that amazes me is that the children are so much more than we were. They're not Allen repeated, or me repeated, or not even him and me. They're something else. I see things in them that I don't know where it comes from, but from God. They outdo me in areas where I would have liked to excel. And to realize that I'm connected to them, that they're a part of me, that is exciting!"

"Then you don't think of them as problems with a capital P?"

"No. Allen worries about travel dangers — bicycles, motorcycles, cars. But so far as ideas are concerned, I know that they think in ways that I didn't think when I was their age. Yet they don't think things that I feel are bad. I know that I have grown so much in my own understandings, and that God is very real to me. But I see Him as real to them, also. They don't always do what I would do, and they do some things that I could not and would not do, but it's not that they're always wrong and I'm always right. I figure that I am I and they are they."

"Don't you have any worries about your kids, other than traffic on the highway and that sort of thing?"

"Yes, of course I have concerns for them, and I pray and tell the Lord just how I feel about them. But I realize He knows more about it than I do, so I ask Him to take care of things the best way. You don't tell Him how to do it! I gave that up a few years ago, because He never did oblige me."

She laughed. "I decided to tell Him what I was thinking about and see if He didn't have something better in mind than I did. And He always did.

"I do lie in bed at night and worry about the children, and wonder what's going to happen. But it's not because they are giving me a hard time. It's that I don't trust the future in this world. I think things are mighty rough. Yet the children amaze me by how they face things that I worry about."

We asked her how she and Allen help their children to face pagan philosophies in the world in which they live, and she told us that they have tried to give their children other reasons than simply that the Bible says something is wrong.

"I believe that if God said something, He had a reason for it," she told us. "God said these things are wrong because they are harmful and damaging. They didn't become wrong because He said it. If something has been labeled as sin, there must have been a reason. If we know the reason, we tell them. If we don't know the reason, we let them know we are still looking and hope they will, too. If God didn't say it, and there isn't a reason, I'm with them to drop it."

Doris had been doing most of the talking because it was she whom I was interviewing, but I asked both of them a question which I find interesting and varied with different couples.

"How do you feel that you complement each other?"

Doris thought a minute before she replied, "Allen has such a steady, quiet faith, and such good judgment, and my faith is so up-and-downish and my judgment so poor. I don't know where I'd be without someone like that. He's been a good father, discipline-wise, and also in making the children feel important. I would have spoiled them terribly if it weren't for him."

Allen found it harder to articulate his feelings. "Doris complements me greatly, but I find it hard to put into words."

Doris helped him. "I do all of his worrying for him."

When we talked about their pattern for living, Allen said that he was the head of the house, and Doris confirmed that he was and that she wanted him to be, for her sake as well as the children's.

"Equality is a funny word," she said, "for though I feel perfectly equal, when people talk about it with a capital E, it makes me mad. And so far as liberation is concerned, I was set free quite a few years ago when I first committed my life to Christ. And I'm even freer now than I was then."

Doris felt that her main role as a Christian woman was as a helper and encourager, though she felt that she often fell short of this ideal. Allen interrupted to say that she did a good job of it.

Doris added that she thought women should be women. Although she found teaching most rewarding and hoped to influence some young lives in the years to come, she still preferred to be thought of as a homemaker and mother who incidentally worked outside the home, rather than a career woman who incidentally was a homemaker and mother. She liked to think of herself as a "homemaker plus."

Doris went on to tell that she enjoys doing many different things and was taken aback the year before when her fellow-teachers could hardly believe she knew how to crochet. "My interests are surely not limited to books, committee meetings, and reports," she explained.

Thinking back to her years of preparation for her lifework, Doris has no regrets. Although she did not accomplish all the things she once envisioned when she wrote to Allen, her life has been full of opportunities to influence through public speaking, leading retreats, devotional writing, and teaching.

And of course there are the children. "My main

purpose and goal in life, besides being Allen's wife and making life meaningful, is to see my kids get established somewhere in something. Right now I have trouble seeing beyond that," she admitted.

"I feel that I am now seven people instead of one person," she went on. "I don't ever expect to be one person again. When the children leave, five of me will be gone. When I am gone, six of me will still be left. Maybe I need an identity crisis!"

But Doris also has personal goals. "I asked myself today if it is important to me to be a successful person," she said thoughtfully. "And I decided that the emphasis should be on *person*. I want to be a real, whole person, understanding and helpful. And enabled for whatever task is handed to me."

Doris thought of her faults and struggles and shared with us how she had just the other day talked one problem over with a son, who had calmly agreed that her self-analysis was correct.

This, however, did not discourage our friend, who knows that growth does not take place without patience, prayer, and work. And as I watch her family grow and mature, I also see a homemaker plus, one who is enjoying every chapter of her life as it comes and looking for more joys in the days ahead.

Billie Ruth Schlank: It would be nice to see, but it's nice to be blind, too. We have a lot of love in this house.

She Sees with Her Heart

It was on a visit to my parents' home, near Washington, D.C., that I met Billie Ruth Schlank, and the more I learned about her, the more I wanted to ring her doorbell.

When I listened to Billie Ruth talk, I noticed that she spoke casually of *watching* TV, *looking at* a new house, *reading* a book, or *seeing* a truth. But, although Billie saw a great deal more in life than many people I have met, she did not see with her eyes. For both she and her husband, Alan, were born blind.

So It was that I made an appointment to stop in and visit with Billie Ruth one evening after she had put six-year-old Ruth Ann to bed. Dad and I opened the gate of the anchor fence and spoke a few words with Prince, the German shepherd who greeted us. My father introduced me to Prince and assured him that I was "OK." Then we climbed Billie Ruth's front steps and were welcomed by an attractive 27-year-old brunette, who cordially invited us in.

"This is a terrible time to call on you," I apologized, noticing the packing boxes around the living room, for Billie Ruth and her family were moving.

She did not seem flustered about our appearance, however. During the years that she and Alan were neighbors to my parents, they frequently dropped in on each other, if for no other reason than to have my father read them their mail. Just the day before I had seen Alan, braillewriter on his knees, writing off some important data which my father read aloud to him.

"I spent the whole day at the new house," Billie told us, as we found chairs. "It's pretty hard to see what it's going to look like. It's so empty and echoey."

As she began speaking a clock struck 8:00. "Our clock plays to us every fifteen minutes," she smiled, "and we like it. You might look at the wall and see there's a picture there, but we prefer clocks that chime and sculpture we can feel, because they speak to us. Modern furniture I don't like — it's very square, very straight, very nondescript, whereas French Provincial furniture, which we are buying for the new house, has feeling and a different shape to it. I really like that sort of thing."

I asked her more about the new house, and she told me that it would be a split-level with living room, dining room, kitchen, two bedrooms, and a bath upstairs and a recreation room, two bedrooms, a bath, and a laundry downstairs.

"Is doing the laundry a problem to you?" I wondered. "No," she laughed. "Some people have decided that I am incompetent with stairs, but stairs don't bother me at all.

"We bought this new house, which is in Arlington, Virginia, mostly with the idea of my being able to get out more. It is only three blocks from our church, for instance, and Mormons are always very active. We are a lay church, highly organized, and I like being involved. Then, too, our home will be within two blocks of a bus line, and shopping will be simple."

"How did you meet Alan?" I wanted to know. "In a school for the blind?"

"Well, yes and no," she told me. "I am from Arizona, Alan from Tacoma, Washington, and we first met in San Francisco when we were taking language aptitude tests under a program for blind persons sponsored by the Department of Health, Education, and Welfare. I was nineteen, the age when everyone wants to do his own thing and not his parents' things. By the time we came to Washington both of us were acclimated in mobility and daily living skills."

"Where did you learn these skills?"

"Primarily in living. You know, when you're going to live in the world, you're going to move around. They do have courses to teach you to use a cane, but neither Alan nor I had had much need for a cane before we came to D.C. My Mommy usually took me places in the car, for instance.

"But coming to Washington was a great experience for me, because I had been too dependent on Mommy. In Phoenix I had attended a high school for the blind, as well as Arizona State University for two years. Now at Georgetown University I had to be independent, and I'll never be sorry."

"Did you have help in learning to be independent?" I asked.

"A lot of it was desire. But there were thirty of us who were blind who came to Georgetown as part of the language program. We lived in apartments within eight or ten blocks of school, and six of us girls lived in the same house, taking our turn at cooking, cleaning, and other chores. Three of the group were very independent, and the rest of us learned from them. I learned a great deal from my roommate."

"And this is when you started dating Alan?"

"Right. He was working on his master's in Russian, and he liked languages. I did not. We started dating after we had been here a year and a half, dated three months, became engaged for another three or four months, and then got married."

My father had been quiet up to now, but at this point he asked, "How did you and Alan know you were in love when you couldn't see each other?"

Billie Ruth laughed. "Love is really a feeling. It's not the physical appearance that makes the difference. My husband probably likes me because I'm vivacious and he is quiet. I really feel sorry for the not-so-cute girls in normal society. Society is unfair, and often they don't have a chance."

Although Alan and Billie Ruth had come to Georgetown to work on languages, Billie never enjoyed the study and dropped out of school after her marriage. Alan, too, eventually changed his field. He decided that he did not want to work on a PhD and was attracted to a computer school.

"When Ruth Ann was two-and-a-half, I decided I would also like to learn computers and I have been working now for the past three years," she added.

"But I understand you're quitting for a while." Billie Ruth had made no secret of her expectations. A second baby was on the way, and she was glad.

"While we're talking about being at home," I mentioned, "I have a lot of questions about how you manage your household. For instance, do you have a certain place you put such ingredients as salt and baking soda when you are working in the kitchen?"

"Yes, but I also go by the feel of the box or tin, and particularly the smell. One time I attended a baby shower where they had a smelling contest, with various spices wrapped up for guessing. I had no trouble identifying them all. And I think I'm a better cook because of this. Your smell goes along with your taste. My husband, too, sometimes suggests adding some flavor to a dish. Cooking is great fun."

As she told this I remembered my mother relating how, when she once returned home from hospitalization, Billie Ruth and Alan had come in the back door, deposited a delicious layer cake on the kitchen table, and then proceeded to the bedroom where she was recuperating.

"I'm a miserable housekeeper though," Billie went on, "but I believe I would be if I had sight." She chuckled mischievously.

"How can you tell?" Dad and I wanted to know.

"Oh, you never get everything totally picked up.

You get one room picked up and then you go into another room and someone's pulled everything off the shelves, and you think, 'Oh, great,' I don't get any pleasure out of cleaning the walls because they never feel dirty. But one thing I enjoy, and that is carrying my cassette recorder from room to room and 'reading' books while I work. Who likes to scrub floors and think about nothing, when you can scrub floors and have your mind challenged! If I read a good book, I am stimulated for many hours or days of good thought."

"Are there any hazards you must avoid in keeping house?" I asked.

Her response was immediate and definite.

"If there are hazards, you remove them. If there are problems, you solve them. When there is a small child in the house I remove items which might be a problem. I don't like always to be saying 'no, no.' "

Dad took the opportunity to ask something he had always wondered about. "Billie, you always look so nice. How do you select your clothes?"

"I take a friend shopping with me," she responded, "and sometimes I change and take another one, for variety. Then Ruth Ann has a strong color sense, and she often chooses her own clothes."

"How do you know what kind of store you are entering?"

"By smell, you can tell a grocery story or a shoe store by the way it smells."

"How then do you know what colors you are selecting from the closet? Do you arrange your clothes by color?"

36

"I would, if it weren't for Ruth Ann. But with her around, it is not necessary."

"Do you depend on Ruth Ann for very much?"

"No, we are careful not to expect a great deal of her. Of course, if her job this week is to set the table, she'd better do it, that's for sure. This is part of growing up and discipline. And we expect her to come up with the colors, but she doesn't mind this. When she is ready for college, we will insist that she go away from home and become independent. If you live with your parents all the time, you never become a real personality."

"Does Ruth Ann feel that you are different from other parents?"

"Oh, yes, sometimes she says, 'But I wish you weren't blind. Do you wish you weren't blind?' And I say, 'Oh, well, it would be nice to see, but then it's nice to be blind, too. We have all this love in our house, and maybe you get to do lots of things that you wouldn't otherwise. What other kid can tell every kind of bus in the city by its color?"

"Have you ever hired help?"

"I have tried, but good hired help is hard to find. But when the baby comes, we will of course need some help for a little while."

"You mean, to prepare the formula, for instance?"

"Oh, no, we are going to nurse! I think that's the best thing for the baby and the best for you, and you don't have to sterilize things all the time. Not only that, but I find that the most frustrating chore for me is feeding a baby with a spoon. I feel that if I can breast-feed the first six months, cuddling the baby, I'll

37

be happier and the baby will feel very held and very loved. And it really carries over, if you communicate with them in this way."

"How long do you feel that this is important, this method of communication?"

"Even now, in church, my little girl wants to sit on my lap. But I'll have to soon put an end to it, because my lap is getting smaller! Sometimes I have suggested to Ruth Ann that she sit on the bench like the other children, but she makes the excuse that she can see better this way. Since she is used to being held, I will have to continue it after the baby is born until she no longer feels the need for it. But she won't feel pushed out, and the new baby will get the same kind of holding that Ruth Ann got. I won't have time for much else during this time, but I feel it is time well spent."

"I notice that you have worked away from home some of the time since Ruth Ann was born. What is your philosophy? Do you feel a mother should spend a lot of time with her children to the exclusion of other things?"

"I have mixed feelings about this. When we were broke and I could not afford baby-sitters, I found it difficult to be at home all the time. Also, I found that when our little girl was small, we had to concentrate on her movements every moment that she was awake. This was very fatiguing. Then when she was asleep, I had to work at such jobs as ironing, which was not safe to do when she was up and about. Until she was old enough to reason with, she could have chewed on a cord, pulled at what I was ironing, or pulled the iron off the ironing board."

"You who are blind have to develop other faculties, such as listening, to a much greater degree, don't you?"

"Right. The ordinary person doesn't have to develop the high degree of concentration that we do. And with a small child, there is no feedback to reward one for his trouble. Oh, you love it when the first tooth comes in, and they sit up and laugh, and all those wonderful things that working mothers don't have a chance to enjoy. But you also need some time to do your own thing.

"I tend to think that it's because of my gregarious nature and my need for involvement that I need time for my own interests. And fortunately, with the new baby, I will be able to afford a sitter for maybe an hour a day."

"What do you do, when you do your own thing?"

"As I said before, the new house is located close to shopping centers, and only a block and a half from the recreation center. Who knows, I just might teach a class a morning or two a week after the baby is a few months old. Another project I have in mind is taking a modern math course so that I can better understand when my little girl starts with her math."

I laughed. "That's surely better than I have done," I admitted.

"And then I love to write programs for the computer, to cook, to read (talking books and braille), and to knit (I just took a knitting course recently). I like to be organized and to carry out things. I like to teach my Sunday school class. In our church you do what you are asked to do and they say, with the Spirit of the Lord, you can accomplish anything."

"Billie Ruth," I broke in, "one time when I was visiting my parents, I heard you say that you were trying to help another blind person to see that she didn't need to be so helpless. I have often wondered, what did you do when you helped her?"

"Working with the blind is one of my major-major activities. But I work in person-to-person encounters, because classwork is too competitive, and I would rather help a person see what a cool individual he really is.

"I was president of the Twin County Federation for the Blind here in Maryland two and a half years; I loved every moment of it. We do many good things through this organization — get Civil Service exams onto cassette tapes, help people to become independent, help persons to find jobs, speak to groups in behalf of the blind, work for the education of blind children, improve library services, and work with legislating social security benefits. You know, we have to 'buy sight' to drive, to do some of our shopping, and to acquire housekeeper services.

"But getting back to your question about what I try to do for individual people. I try to teach them that, first of all, they're just people like anyone else, with responsibilities they would have whether they could see or not, and the world doesn't owe them a living. They owe a contribution, instead, to the world. I try to teach them to read braille so that a woman, for instance, could read recipes, follow patterns, read a good book, and follow instructions of any kind. I would teach them to use a stove, not because they wouldn't know how, but because they would be afraid of it. If they were young, I'd take them skating to give them self-confidence, and I'd suggest some sport they thought they couldn't do — horseback-riding, sharpshooting, anything challenging.

"I might ask them over to cook steaks on a backyard grill, and they'd have to build their own fire. We just wouldn't eat until they did. If a fellow was a good gardener, I'd learn from him, because I'm planning to try some gardening. I'm going to plant some double-dwarf fruit trees so that I can spray them myself. I love putting fruit in the deepfreeze and that sort of thing."

"How many people do you think you have helped, on a person-to-person basis?" I asked.

"I have no idea."

"Say, Dad," I suggested, "if you need a program at church sometime, there's your speaker."

Billie Ruth laughed. "Wind me up!"

While we were talking, Prince meandered across the room, almost interfering with the cord to the tape recorder. Billie Ruth stopped to pat him and tell him what an exceptional dog he is.

"You know, he's not a Seeing-Eye dog," she explained. "He's just an ordinary German shepherd who's been to obedience school and who thinks that he owns our yard. But when he's lying on the floor and hears us coming, he knows we can't see and so he takes his tail and goes, 'thump, thump, thump,' so we won't step on him. I appreciate it that Mr. Good introduces repairmen and other workers who come to the yard. otherwise Prince wouldn't let them in."

"I have a friend with another handicap who feels that she meets discrimination at times. Do you feel discriminated against, Billie Ruth?"

"I sure do," Billie clipped. "There is discrimination all over. I went into a dime store one day and was told that I could not shop there. I replied that it was a public place, and the manager told me that he didn't want me stumbling over merchandise. I told him that he shouldn't have merchandise where you could stumble over it, and he ordered me out. And people have a tendency to treat you like you're stupid or something, sometimes directing their questions to someone else when they take your order in a restaurant, for example.

"Actually, though, I consider blindness a nuisance, but I wouldn't call it a handicap," she summarized.

Listening to this active, involved homemaker, I had to agree with her, for she had not allowed her blindness to reduce her effectiveness; perhaps it enhanced it. And she did see, with her fingers (*I check things out with my hands*), with her ears (*a busy street is not a hazard, for there are traffic signals*), with her smell (*I can tell what kind of store I am entering*), with her taste (*it's so much fun to cook*), with her bodily contacts (*I communicate with my children by holding them*). And as I thought about it, I felt she had an extra sense. For she had said, "Love is a feeling," and any woman knows that this is true. Billie Ruth feels deeply, and she "sees" with her heart.

42

Ruth Remple: In some areas John excels; in others I do. We try to interact responsibly with each other and society.

And the Two Became One

I was really impressed at Ruth Rempel's wedding. Her husband, John, is a Canadian of German background, and therefore some of the music, a few of the prayers, and the elaborate reception smorgasbord, followed by a program, reflected the traditions of his culture. On the other hand, Ruth, the daughter of missionary parents, had lived her life in two completely different cultures, Indian and American, transplanted often enough in her twenty-two years, that her roots did not have a chance to penetrate deeply into either soil. As I watched her, young and blond and tender, lean over in the receiving line to kiss a little relative, I thought of the enrichment which John and Ruth would bring to each other.

Ruth was still a bride of a year when my husband and I rang the doorbell of their apartment. Now that Ruth, the youngest daughter of Dr. and Mrs. J. G. Yoder, had married, the older couple has returned to the mission field on an indefinite basis, this time stationed in Nepal. Since Ruth and John were spending the year in the Goshen, Indiana, area, they took up residence in the basement apartment of the Yoder home, maintained by the missionaries for the occasional furloughs sprinkled throughout their career.

As John let us in, we crossed a bearskin, then admired several leopard skins in other rooms of the apartment. Ruth explained that her father had shot these animals himself, and many more. Other than that the apartment was not unusual; simple and efficient, it was not too difficult for a young working couple to manage in their hours off. Ruth was temporarily employed in the doctor's office where her father practiced on furloughs, and John, a seminary graduate, edited a periodical for college students and worked as a research assistant.

My husband and I felt at home with the Rempels, as John and Virgil had cooperated on the student newssheet for a number of years. John, much younger than my husband, had often shared his feelings and views on many subjects, including marriage. John is a thinker and he likes to articulate his thoughts.

With the wedding still fresh in my mind, I asked John about his background, since that had given the wedding such a distinctiveness. I knew that, although his parents spoke German and were of German descent, they had fled to Canada, along with many other religious refugees from the Ukraine of Russia, following the trauma and persecution of the Revolution.

John told us how his parents had come over from Russia in their teens during the 1920s, how their way of life had been destroyed, and how they tenaciously carried with them what they could and sought to rediscover that way of life in Canada. Since his mother was ill much of the time, this compounded their sense of tenuousness and appreciation for family and community.

"I was instilled with a sense of tradition and custom as a way of giving meaning and continuity to life, which was often threatened by tragedy," he said. "To have arrived at any religious landmarks such as baptism, communion, weddings, and funerals, seemed an act of the grace of God."

Ruth had been participating with her eyes as John described his religious heritage which had been so much a part of the wedding itself. I looked at her as I asked, "Wasn't the smorgasbord reception sort of German, also? We usually get by with punch and cake."

She laughed and explained that the dishes her parents served were not unusual: ham, chicken and aspic salad, and a variety of other salads along with the hot bread and coffee. But John added, "Ruth's family wasn't used to that kind of reception and did it out of affection for us Having a whole meal was Germanic, as was the program afterward, where various people got up and spoke with an earnest lightheartedness, and there were musical numbers. My mother told me that my father had worked for months on the talk that he gave, since he was sure after meeting Ruth that I would marry her. Ruth's father and a sister-in-law also gave short talks, and I spoke briefly."

"Ruth," I inquired, "what in the wedding came from your tradition?"

She thought for a moment. "That's a rough one, partly because I don't know what traditions are in my background. Tradition and historical roots and all this have meant a lot less to our family."

"Were you living in India all of your growing-up years before you went to college?"

"No, I lived there until I was five, and since I didn't know English very well, I had real adjustment problems when my parents returned to the States to see my older sisters through college. I don't think I became completely adjusted until I was in the fifth or sixth grade. I wanted to shake off every attachment I had with India, to forget the language, and the people, and the village, and everything."

"You wanted to belong in your American surroundings? And then when you were in the sixth grade you returned to India?"

"That was the only stretch when Mom and Dad were in the States for any length of time," she remembered. "My two sisters had spent most of their lives in India and had graduated from high school there."

"You were the baby?"

"Right. And my family didn't know quite what to do with me. I was rebelling against everything they held to so strongly. When we returned to India, I spent four years at Woodstock, a boarding school, and that was a real period of growing up for me. It was the first time I was away from my parents for most of the year, and the peer group pressures are really of ultimate importance during those years. Then, when you're together all the time, they double in their importance."

As Ruth evaluated these years, however, she concluded she was discovering who she was during this time, and what she was to be. She gradually saw what India meant to her physician father and her mother, who served as hospital dietitian and in literacy work, both in India and Nepal.

"The biggest impression had been made on me in those six years in the States," Ruth explained, "and I thought in terms of that all the time, and thought my mom and dad belonged there, too. Finally I realized who my parents were, and that their life was much more in India than in the States. Coming to the States was just a rest for them, until they got started again. And they wanted to be sure that each of their girls could graduate from college.

"I speculate a lot," she went on. "Missionary kids in boarding schools have many adjustment problems, but I was fortunate during my most formative years to be with my parents. Though I fought the idea, I knew my residence in the States wasn't a permanent thing, so I was sort of prepared for moving on. I didn't feel snatched and tossed about. Then when I returned to India, my parents placed a lot of emphasis on the girls being self-sufficient when they got out of school, much more than on getting married and settling down. They made sure we could take care of ourselves. My one sister became a doctor, the other a teacher, and both were able to be independent. But the last year I spent in India, my sophomore year in college, I found all that emphasis on self-sufficiency challenged by the Indian girls."

That was one thing I wanted to find out from Ruth. How had living in India influenced her view on the role of women?

"My Indian friends were taught that they should be prepared to be women in the home, raising children, and being submissive. That was the year I was most independent, traveling on my own and things like that, which I hadn't had an opportunity to do before."

John put in, "One thing I remember that you mentioned was that living with Indian peers, the quiet, subservient, withdrawn role of the Indian woman impressed you."

"Yes," Ruth said, "in the very traditional homes."

"How did you feel about this?" I pushed.

"We talked and talked about this for hours," she said. "And I guess the thing that most impressed me was that the girls were satisfied with it. They didn't resent their role in the least, and the same with planned marriages. Few of my friends felt they would be capable of selecting their own husbands. They left it to their parents' judgment and were glad it was that way. That was a revelation to me."

"Did you argue with them?"

Ruth giggled. "Back and forth and back and forth."

"Did it confirm you in your convictions? Which way did it swing you?"

"Well, it showed me that there was more than one way to look at it. It also showed me that in some ways I didn't really belong to either culture. What they saw in the American woman — the free and loose and totally independent kind of thing — that did not appeal to me. There is something very strong in the gentleness and willingness to submit freely in the Indian woman, that I appreciated and was drawn to. But yet I knew girls whose sisters had real struggles when their husbands refused to let them associate with their own families. I couldn't believe that they should submit in such cases without even arguing about it."

"When you were in America you felt like an Indian, and when you were in India you felt like an American?"

"Yes. The year I spent in an Indian college, I was definitely in the minority. Although there were 500 Indian girls, there were only two Americans. I remember the first two weeks I was there I spent in the dispensary, and I was really, really lonely. I was sick, and I wasn't allowed visitors, and I didn't know anybody. It was during the hot season, the grounds were overgrown, and there were monkeys sliding up and down the water pipes right outside my window.

"The first night I was out of the dispensary the Indian girls invited me to spend the night with them, and I felt it was a good chance to get acquainted. They bombarded me with questions about what my parents were doing in India, what on earth missionaries thought they were doing there in the first place, about the peace convictions of my church (Mennonite), the American policy in Vietnam, and how I could reconcile those two positions. They represented

British colonialism, and antagonisms were strong. I really didn't know how to answer half the questions they asked me."

"You had pretty well gone through your identity crisis before that year in college, hadn't you?"

"To some extent. But not as great as in that year. At Woodstock I struggled to find I was an individual and had to find out what I stood for alone, separated from my family. My college year in India was harder. I didn't know what to identify myself with."

I had drawn out Ruth and John on their backgrounds because they were so different, but now I wanted to know how they were getting on in pooling their interests, merging their lives, adjusting their values. Of course, I knew that they did a lot of thinking and that they would not quickly tell me that all of this was none of my business!

"Then how," I asked, "did you get together?"

"We met when we were invited to give entertainment at an Indian supper," Ruth responded. "That was soon after I came back to the States, and I played my *sitar* in a musical number with a fellow who played a *thabla,* another Indian instrument. John and I got to talking about our travel experiences."

I knew also that after her graduation and before their marriage Ruth and John had spent some time in Florida, taking part in a Christian commune, an experiment in small-group church life. John had been asked to coordinate the experiment, and Ruth had joined the group later, teaching school in Sarasota and getting better acquainted with John.

"I wanted to know him better than I would by just dating him and talking with him. This experiment was something he was interested in enough to give a year of his life to. It was important to him."

John described how the group — a dry wall contractor, a teacher, a youth worker, an editor, and others — grew into a community, sharing in an informal atmosphere. Some lived on the second floor of a vegetable warehouse. All enjoyed the out-of-doors and ideal weather.

"The simpleness of the way we lived, the lack of competition with one another, the newness, almost childlikeness of our existence — I think some of these things carried over to our honeymoon," he told us.

The couple were eager to tell us about their honeymoon in Europe. "It was absolutely delightful," John said. "We were fortunate in having accommodations in a friend's home in Paris, but again, it was completely unpretentious. We didn't go to a single nightclub. Instead, we wandered around the back streets of the area where we lived and took the tram into the city to see the sights, taking our lunch along and speaking our broken French."

There was more. They had hitchhiked through some parts of Europe, visited points of historical and religious interest in France and Switzerland, showed each other places they had seen on earlier trips, and joined friends on a visit to Berlin. Hitchhiking through sections of England and Scotland, they had visited friends of the Yoders in Glasgow and ended their "impossible journey" on the island of Skye.

"Your whole life has been an impossible journey," I observed.

"Yes," John agreed. "It dispels the gloom of uncertainties that seem to beset us. Both of us, when we recall the journey so far, are very, very grateful."

In recalling the honeymoon, Ruth said, "It would have been easy, if we had stayed at home, to go plunging on our ways. It would have taken awhile to come to terms with our widely different interests without a lot of frustration if we hadn't spent time away and seen them from a distance."

I knew Ruth's fields of interest, but not how she planned to pursue her psychology and English literature.

"I would have liked to have gone on to grad school in clinical psychology," she mentioned, "either counseling in a school or working in a mental health clinic."

Knowing that the next plans on the Rempel agenda were a summer working on an historical film in Ontario and a year in Berlin, we inquired as to whether she had given up her personal ambitions.

"No, I just have to wait and see how it fits in," she explained. "If it doesn't work out in an institution, my training definitely will be valuable in the home and with friends, and things like that."

"You're not uptight about it, then?"

"No, no."

Virgil, a friend of many graduate students, wondered if she had given up the idea of grad school for good.

She was relaxed in her response. "Given it up immediately, yes, because so far it has become a secondary interest and there are other things I want to do next year. Maybe the next year it will be a possibility."

John interrupted to say that while he would be studying in an old university in Berlin under a scholarship from the World Council of Churches, plans were hazy at the moment for Ruth. Ruth candidly shared the problem which this indefiniteness made for her.

"At first, when we began plotting the trip, it seemed definitely that this is where John's interests tied in. He was really, really excited about it. But I just couldn't see where I could possibly fit in. And you know, it's no longer assumed in the culture we're growing up in that the woman's interests are always submitted to the man's and that she automatically follows him. It was a real struggle for me to decide whether it was honest to give up my career interests or my hopes of sometime returning to India."

"I think there are two factors," John pointed out, "that have made our life together demanding and rewarding. One is that we are both strong-willed and that we have strong interests. I think that Ruth has worked them out more thoroughly than I have, but I suppose I have to admit that at times I assume my interest in theology and the life of the church has moral superiority over other kinds of work. The other thing is that both of us have had many friends and have been allowed positions of leadership, and the affection shown us included an indulgence in terms of the things we wanted. Then, when you bring two people like that together, there's a certain amount of confusion!"

They were answering some of my questions before I asked them. I turned to Ruth. "Then you take by faith that you will find something rewarding to do in Berlin?"

"We struggle, and struggle, and still struggle with that," she replied. "Part of it for me was to realize that even if I did not immediately plunge into grad school and my books, when you enter a new culture where things are so different, your eyes are really opened to people and yourself, and you become much more aware of how different cultures develop people in different ways. I had to admit that, whether I knew exactly what I'll be doing or not, I'm interested in going. It's not a place where our interests are polarized, where there's something for John and nothing for me."

We had discussed how Ruth's Indian background caused her to think deeply on the role of women. I wanted more of her ideas.

"Do you have any resentment toward man as a doer in society and woman as a sustainer, and accepting a supportive role in the marriage relationship?"

Again, she was honest. "I guess I would have to say yes. I suspect my awareness of that is heightened right now. It's brought out in almost everything you read. John's is a culture that says that man is dominant and rightly so, and he's the authority in many ways."

"John," I asked, "Does your background complicate this issue?"

"Well, my father accepted the dominant role as part of his culture, and there was no equivocation about whether a man provided for his family in the broad sense of the word. Also, there was little equivocation about whether he was the undisputed leader. The woman followed and baked and took care of the children and things like that, and my mother did this and. . . ."

"And was happy doing it," I finished for him.

"Basically she was happy, yes."

Again, the four of us discussed role expectation, and John philosophized that his background was less aware of the psychological dimensions of life than Ruth's. Although he reacted to its rigidity of outlook, at the same time he was not ashamed of his past and wanted to take some of its values into the present.

"You kids have some advantage over people our age," Virgil remarked, "I suspect we entered marriage without so much awareness of role expectation being created from our backgrounds. We sort of stumbled into the thing."

"We didn't think it through like this," I agreed.

"And yet," Ruth said, "while we no longer assume roles, we still have a tendency to suspect assumed roles in the other person because we're so conscious of the fact that we don't want to assume them."

"Do you think, Ruth, that women in America are oppressed?" I questioned.

"I think that needs to be qualified. In some areas, yes. Perhaps more so in some of our communities where roles are so clearly defined. The woman does not question the fact that her person may be swallowed up and her interests are always secondary."

"I think we all agree with that."

"Do you have any other 'beefs' about society's treatment of women?"

"I guess I have a beef, too, about the present movement, which almost assumes that woman wants to get away from her responsibilities in the home and raising children. If that is where her interests lie, she needs liberating, so that that is a possibility. And men need liberating, too."

"Do you think equality is an ideal?"

"I don't know exactly what that means. There are areas in which I know John excels, and vice versa. Equality is how we use our various talents and act out our responsibility to each other, the home, and society."

We talked over the importance of interdependence in marriage, as opposed to the emphasis on individuality in our society.

"Ruth, do you feel that you are experiencing growth in finding your own identity? Does marriage help you develop your talents?" I wanted to know.

"Yes, yes," she emphasized. "I think that a person, before he enters marriage, has to have an identity as an individual, and a lot of the basic struggles of 'who I am' conquered. But I think they are looked at and readjusted in marriage. If there's a clear enough idea that the people involved don't threaten each other, this can be a very growing thing, and there's something greater formed than the individual personalities of the two."

"One thing I would say," John thought aloud, "is that the marriage relationship is so unreserved and unending, that it opens a part of life that is otherwise invisible and unknown. Ruth and I have had many beautiful friendships, and in a way the close relationships in life are on a continuum, culminating in the marriage relationship. But in no other relationship does one give his whole life to another person, for always. In a dorm situation, for instance, if you are on the outs a bit, you avoid each other. And you don't pool your money or your plans for the summer. I think we have almost an instinct, a very deep sense of the optimum level in a friendship, beyond which we won't go.

"But it's just not like that in marriage, where the unreservedness and unendingness take the shape of not leaving each other, and going everywhere together. In marriage we share everything from brushing our teeth (very mundane) to waking up in the morning (which can be very beautiful). In marriage you don't set up ideal balances. You cope with what comes, you receive what is given, the beautiful and the mundane. I suppose at first this is a shock, but it's a very strengthening thought in a sense that there is a willingness and the possibility to even attempt to live in this way."

"So the ideal relationship between man and wife is an acceptance of the whole?"

"Yes, and it goes beyond all relationships that are temporary and have reservations."

Virgil said, "There is probably a good reason to

believe that this committed relationship in the end is the only one where growth takes place, where you do not walk out on the nitty-gritty problems that need to be solved in order to make the relationship function."

"I would hope, however," John said, "that this strength in giving would carry over into other friendships."

Ruth had made a similar point earlier, when she had said, "One thing we have become very much aware of is that even as a couple, we're not self-sufficient. We depend a great deal on close friends and family for counsel and guidance." Now she added, "There's obviously a vulnerability that grows in marriage, that, if it's betrayed, could break a person. As long as it isn't, the promise and the knowledge that one is loved and accepted, even in the most mundane areas, can open one to attempt to build that kind of relationships elsewhere."

We had been delving into the deeper meanings of marriage. I decided to switch to the practical.

"Speaking of mundane things, I want to give you an easier question to answer. How do you divide your housekeeping chores, since both of you are working? Do you have a system?"

They laughed, and one of them quipped, "As the spirit moves."

But Ruth went into more detail. "I like, when I wake up in the morning, to know that I can just lie there and don't have to jump out of bed immediately. And John's a go-getter. He goes out jogging first and then wakes me up. While I'm gathering myself together, he fixes breakfast. Then he goes to work, and I do dishes or meal planning or cleaning before I go to work. Cleaning I usually do since I am fortunate to get home around 4:00 in the afternoon. Then I usually fix supper and John washes the dishes."

While we were talking, John poured us all a cup of tea and served us some European chocolates. When the telephone rang, the couple made a game of racing for it.

"Does role expectation bother you if you help around the house, John?" I asked our host.

"No. Since my mother was often ill, I was used to that. I feel that love allows for this. But I do get irritated sometimes, because I like to be about things that seem more important (as we all do). And I had developed some bachelor habits, being already twenty-six when I married. Sometimes I forget that Ruth can also be irritated by mundane things. Basically, I'm not averse to it."

"How about you, Ruth? Does role expectation bother you when John helps?"

Her quick, merry laughter was self-explanatory. "No. These are things that always seem to get in the way. They are just chores that need to be done. They don't seem to be creative. Now cooking is different."

"Yes," John said, "Ruth will spend hours and hours baking bread that I would say is better than my mother's, and I have a high regard for my mother's cooking."

Ruth went on. "I have a lot of recipe books, and there are other things around the house I like to do, such as decorating, weaving, painting, and writing sometimes. And I do some ceramics."

Of course, one subject could not be ignored. "Do you plan to have a family? Now if you tell me one thing for this book and then turn around and do another, no one will hold you to it," I joked.

"Interestingly enough, that is just what we were talking about. We feel very definitely that for the two of us, even in our development as persons and in our responsibility to each other, raising children is important. Now whether that is having children naturally or adopting them is something we'll still have to work out. The first is always appealing — there is a wonder that accompanies it."

"How do you have this worked into the blueprint for your life?"

"We don't want to have any children until we feel we'll be in one place for at least a year, which hasn't happened yet. I won't expect to have a child and then pass it off and continue on my merry way. One's life changes, and I would have to make the child a primary concern for a while. I think that I would have to center my interests around the child. Now I don't see that as a sacrifice. I don't think people should have children if they think that from then on they will have to sacrifice what they think is best for the two of them or for themselves as individuals. That's where the children get confused."

Virgil noted that the commitment to one's children was like that we had spoken of in marriage.

"Yes, definitely. But not at the expense of the marriage. If the child helps the two of you grow, if the child is someplace where you pool your interests and your ideals in a very conscious way, someone whom both of you can contribute to and benefit from, and you take all the responsibility that goes along with it, that's commitment."

I thought about this couple and the "impossible journey" that had brought them together, spanning three continents and numerous countries. "What would you say is your purpose for traveling this road of life, your dreams for the future?"

There was a long pause, then Ruth said, "I don't know if we have articulated that to each other. One thing that brought us together was the idealism and dedication we both felt to working for God and His people. What all that means, I don't know. We make our plans sort of a year at a time."

"You're a modern couple, world citizens."

"And hopefully, even after we have children, we'll continue to be that way. We hope the security we provide for them in the home will make it possible for them to be mobile."

John added, "I think a comment Ruth made earlier, about interdependence, is important to us: between the two of us, with our friends, and with our church. Being in a company of people who acknowledge this interdependence in our world provides for us the most significant stability, more than staying in one location."

Perhaps the next generation of Rempels will not put down deep roots in one spot of God's universe. But the merger of lives from which they come will guarantee another kind of heritage.

Frances Bontrager: Our goal is to help the retarded child, his parents, and the family to live as normally as possible.

Third Person Singular

When you ring Fran's doorbell, you pull a string on a ceramic owl, which rings a clapper bell.

"I have this thing about owls," Fran smiles, as she lets you in. "My girlfriend and I liked the poem about the wise old owl and began sending one another cards and later little objects in the shape of an owl. Other friends found out about this and added to my collection."

Owls are not the only distinctive feature about the Early American bungalow which Frances Bontrager and her housemate, Laura Metzler, renovated in a woodsy section of Goshen, Indiana. Most people remember the tree.

It seems that the girls needed a two-car garage, but did not want to sacrifice a large tree on the west side of their house. While they were considering the choice, the thought occurred to them that they could have both if they would build a screened-in patio around that tree. Checking with a botanist, they learned that they were on the right side of a nearby dam for protection against tornadoes, and that the engineering feat would be possible if water spouts were installed and enough room allowed for the tree to sway.

"Since we bought the lot because of the trees, we hated to destroy a tree," Fran told me.

Another special feature about Fran and Laura's house is the large dining room-living room area with the sunken fireplace. Students frequently fill this room from nearby Goshen College, who know that they can come for fun and fellowship. Besides those who are invited and entertained, there are also those who make reservations and do their own entertaining.

Fran (also known as Bonnie) explained that students frequently bring their own refreshments or cook them in the kitchen, perhaps pizza on a chilly evening or a cake on a Sunday afternoon. The house was planned with privacy in two areas, so that the owners could be in one part while the college students could have the living room to themselves. And the homeowners have a few rules.

"If the guys want to use our fireplace for proposing, they have to carry their own firewood!" Fran jokingly told me. "And we've known several couples who have made pretty definite life commitments at our house."

There are four other rules for youth who use Fran and Laura's facilities. When they leave, they must sign their names on a narrow white roller window shade by the door, provided for that purpose, pull the fireplace screen, turn off the lights, and lock the door.

Fran and Laura particularly enjoy entertaining international students, as both of them have served terms abroad in church-sponsored relief efforts. It was at a hospital in Nazareth, Ethiopia, where Fran, an RN, and Laura, a secretary, first met.

"When you are roommates 8,000 miles away from home, you get pretty well acquainted," Fran said. "I liked to do lots of crazy things, and so did Laura. We had a good time.

"That was twenty years ago," she went on, "and at the little rural hospital we nurses had to take a lot of responsibility, sometimes even playing doctor. There are three freshmen at Goshen College whom I helped deliver when I was in Ethiopia."

Fran told about one boy, a recent arrival and son of a lab technician she had known in Nazareth, who was surprised when she began speaking to him in Amharic.

"How long ago were you in Ethiopia?" he asked.

"Look, Samuel, I delivered you!" she responded to the astonished boy.

Since that time, Fran told me, several fellows who came to the house asked, "Are you the lady who delivered Samuel?"

"That usually breaks the ice," she laughed.

The Ethiopian story was only one chapter of Frances Bontrager's varied and interesting life. Born the ninth of ten children, Fran was the only child in the family who received a high school diploma. And that took effort and determination.

"We were allowed to attend high school until we were sixteen," Fran said, "but it was believed that a girl didn't need a high school education to wash diapers, which was what she would end up doing anyway."

Fran, whose home was not far from Buffalo, New York, had other ideas. Although she stayed at home until she was twenty-one, she began completing her high school through correspondence courses. Finishing her high school and nurse's training at a church-related school, she spent two years in relief work in Ethiopia, after which she returned with Laura via the Nile River, the Holy Lands, and an extended tour of European countries.

"Each time I came home from an overseas assignment, I felt depleted and wanted to go back to school," she remembered. Since Fran did not have her BS degree at the time of her return from Ethiopia she went back to college, working in Baltimore summers and for one year following her degree, with children afflicted with cerebral palsy.

Later Frances spent a year getting acquainted with the medical practice in her home community, then responded to a need in northern Haiti, where she helped to set up a rural hospital in an area where 80,000 people had been dependent upon voodoo and witch doctors. After a two-year term of service, she again returned home with an urge for more training. Syracuse University, which was not far from her home, appealed to her because of her interest in nursing and journalism. She decided to go for her master's in nursing, and to study some journalism as a means of enrichment and self-expression. Later chapters in her life have included six years of teaching pediatrics in a college school of nursing and her present position as Director of Nursing Services at Aux Chandelles, a school for retarded children supported by the United Fund.

"I really felt, when I was teaching, that I was just existing," Fran reflected. "Studying, grading papers, preparing class notes, and so on took all my time, and all I got done was to attempt to keep ahead of my students. I guess I'm just not cut out to be a teacher. Interacting with students, though, was very fulfilling."

Her present job, however, is something else, and Fran described with joy her experiences in relating to mentally retarded children and their families, helping them to assess their health needs and adjust to their life circumstances.

"Our goal is to help the child, the parents, and other members of the family to live a normal life as much as possible," Fran summed it up. "When you work with a child, you have to work with the parents and the whole family constellation. And I have found that some parents of retarded children are the strongest and greatest people I have ever met. Their suffering has brought out an intensity of feeling and perception that shallow people will never know."

Fran visits every home, staying close to the family situation as a friend and counselor. Her contacts begin when a family becomes aware that their child is retarded. This may be at birth when a child is diagnosed as a mongoloid, for instance. A doctor will tell the parents to get in touch with Fran, who helps them through the difficult period of adjustment and guides them through their questions.

"Or perhaps I just need to be there and be supportive," she added. "Then I continue to follow the family until the child is ready to be admitted to school. Besides this, I write a lengthy and in-depth assessment of each child's health. And I try to help parents whose child seems to be slow to stimulate the child in various ways and prevent further retardation."

Being a family friend and often the only RN a mother knows personally, furnishes Frances with many opportunities to help. She told me of one mother who called to inquire what she should serve for dinner to a guest on a low-cholesterol diet. A fourteen-year-old boy needed a "big brother," and Fran was able to find a couple who were willing to relieve parents of three retarded children for a night's outing away from home each week. When a mother told Fran that there was no money in the family coffer for much-needed glasses for her boy, Fran knew of a fund that would cover the expense. Sometimes it is necessary to give a lesson in child care to a mother, other times Fran's counsel is needed to help dispel hostilities or fears.

"What is an average day like at Aux Chandelles?" I asked.

"There isn't an average day," Fran replied, then enumerated some of the contacts she had made the week before. "I feel responsible to help interpret the program to the community," she explained, "and I led a tour of mothers who wanted to know more about Aux Chandelles. I met with a minister to talk about the possibility of a summer camp program for retarded children. I met with the other directors. I visited a mother in the hospital who had just had a new baby. With one retarded child, this visit was very crucial for her."

And there was the high school class, assigned to write a report on Aux Chandelles, who called one by one to ask Fran a list of questions such as, "What do you do?"

"What, indeed!" she laughed to me. "How could I tell anyone the answer to that question in a few words?"

"It would be like asking a mother what she does in a day," I observed, then decided that that was a good analogy.

I thought of Fran's little joke, in the beginning of our interview, when she told me that, at a recent reunion, she announced that she had 150 children. Then, with tongue in cheek, she had added, "I hope their father is baby-sitting them while I am here."

But when I went to Aux Chandelles to observe, I decided that, except for the father baby-sitting bit, Fran's statement had not been a joke. Fran truly had 150 children!

As I had lunch in the dining hall and visited the classrooms, I noted that Fran had a first-name, caring relationship with every child she met. She listened intently to whatever the child had to say. She called out to cheer a boy whose walking was improving with practice. She announced to another lad that he could expect his braces by Thursday. She hugged a "birthday girl" whose mother came in later with refreshments for her party. She investigated a possible allergy on one small child's face. She called in a little girl to tape the bottom of her shoes so they wouldn't be so slippery. She laid her hand on the shoulder of a "senior" fellow with a few words of encouragement. She looked with interest at the drawings of some of the older students. And she worried whether one child had warm enough wraps and mittens securely fastened for the bus trip home.

"I'm a troubleshooter," she told me, as we looked in on Speech Therapy, the music room, the gym, the homemaking arts lab, academic classrooms, the vocational wing, and the crafts room.

"After I dictate in the morning I make the rounds and check any problems which the teachers have noticed in the children. I also check attendance records and look into things if a child has been absent for a while."

She explained the objectives which the various teachers had for the children — the developing of hand dexterity and manipulative skills, learning right and left and backward and forward movements through square dancing, expressing their feelings and personalities through art and music, gaining skills in home living and self-care, and, for the older ones, acquiring abilities to earn and become productive citizens. I watched older children address and stuff envelopes for a civic group, weave at a loom, and operate machinery, and I bought a decorative pillow manufactured in their small pillow factory.

"Doesn't it take a lot of patience?" I asked, after Fran had paused to visit with a child just turned four and explained to me on the side that they were still deciding if his problem was all brain damage or was partly emotional and psychological.

"Not really," she said. "It takes instead of objectivity, an observation of the child's abilities, and a caring whether he is living up to his highest potential. Parents often do not realize that a child can do more than he is doing, in feeding himself, for instance."

We gravitated into Fran's office, and she brought out some more of her owl collection.

"The wise old owl," I mused. "Is that where you get all the wisdom you dispense every day?" I had a feeling by this time that there were no problems that Frances could not solve with a little thought.

"Did you have special training for this work, other than becoming an RN?" I queried.

Fran explained that the period when she had worked in Baltimore with children who had cerebral palsy had been invaluable. And teaching pediatrics had given her an understanding of what the norm was in child development so that she could better observe deviations.

"The rest is caring. These children know if you really care. They can spot a phony in a hurry.

"Actually, I have great freedom here," she told me. "I even had the privilege of writing my own job sheet."

"It seems to me that you are pretty fulfilled," I observed, "that you are one of the persons whom you describe in your little book as being 'happily unmarried.' "

I had just finished reading the book which Frances had written at the request of her denominational press titled *The Church and the Single Person.* °

Fran assured me that she was not against marriage, but she felt that happiness was a state of mind rather than a marital state.

"There are frequent times when I'm very aware that I'm single," she said, "that I am a third person singular. But I'm not going to marry anyone I can find, to avoid being single. If I marry, I want someone who isn't looking only for a housekeeper. I'm not denying the fact that sometime in life it would be nice to know what marriage is like, but in the meantime I'm not contemptuous or jealous of married people."

I remembered reading statements in Fran's book such as, "The single girl has a problem only as she allows herself to have one. Each of us is ultimately responsible for his own life. There is vast opportunity for self-fulfillment if you don't become drowned in self-pity. What the single girl does with singlehood is up to her."

"Speaking of fulfillment, did you hear the pastor's prayer Sunday morning? That was really different," Fran laughed. "Often the widows and the aged get prayed for, but never the single adult."

°Frances Bontrager, *The Church and the Single Person*, Herald Press, Scottdale, Pa. 15683, 1969.

"I heard it," I told her, "and I thought, 'I hope Fran is listening.' Now, how did he have that worded?"

"I believe it was something like, 'We thank You for the single adults who find fulfillment in their lives.' "

"What is fulfillment anyway, Fran? We hear so much about it these days. Isn't that sort of a wobbly word?"

"It is a wobbly word," she agreed. "But it has to do with finding meaning in life. And there has to be some kind of satisfying feedback. I think single adults find just as much fulfillment, or more, as many married people."

"Your book certainly helps the married to understand the problems and the feelings of the single person living in a marriage-oriented society," I commented. I had noted the snide and tactless remarks which singles are regularly subjected to, the lack of understanding of their needs and their goals, and the loneliness and aloneness which they often face.

"Do you think things are improving for single people?" I asked.

"Definitely. At least I see changes in my church and community," she said, pointing out that the pastor's prayer, for instance, was a sign of hope. Then Fran told me of a little incident that had taken place on Sunday morning as she entered the church. A husband whose wife was working in the nursery had to care for his two children during church and jokingly suggested Fran help him. The three-year-old told her father, "We ought to sit with Bonnie because she doesn't have a daddy."

"Now she had more insight than many adults," Fran

chuckled. "Some of my married friends never think of going anywhere with me until their husbands are away. But I am alone all the time."

"How about friendships?" I asked, remembering Fran's emphasis in her book on the importance of friends, old and young, married and unmarried, male and female. She had said, "Women need men, and men need women, just as each sex needs continued friendship with their own sex. . . . Single persons also need contacts with the opposite sex to keep socially stimulated."

Fran felt fortunate in her career, in the stimulating conversations which she sometimes enjoyed with male fellow-workers. She appreciated her friends of both sexes in personal, professional, and church experiences. But she longed for more contact with families.

We had talked before about the need for extended families in a day when many of us are separated from natural grandparents, aunts, uncles, and cousins. Children need other adult models besides their parents with whom they can relate in their maturing years. Fran felt that here was a need that single adults could fill, at the same time meeting a need in their own lives for family relationships. After all, the church itself should be a family, she felt, but often the church's emphasis on family activities did not include the single person.

"In spite of my convictions on the subject, I don't feel that I have been very successful in relating to families I know," Fran mentioned. "Having come from a large family, I enjoy children, and I would like so much to be part of a family, to really feel involved. I can do fine if I invite children to my house, but I am only invited for special, dress-up occasions instead of the everyday family experiences. I would prefer being invited for leftovers and children's chatter. I wouldn't want to intrude on the intimate aspects of a family's life, but I do need a family."

I thought of all the enriching experiences woven into Fran's life, many of which her married friends could well envy in their more routinized existence. Independent living was a life-style which allowed for all sorts of new experiences, travel to exotic places, innovative activities, acquaintance with a wide variety of persons, specialized Christian service. And there was her intense involvement at Aux Chandelles. You didn't have to be with Fran long to catch some of the spice and challenge of her days.

Fran was honest and open, however, about other alternatives. "Someone recently told me that I am really a career person," she smiled, "and I said, 'Don't let them kid you. If I met the right person, I'd be glad to quit in a hurry.' This friend pointed out to me that I might not be able to stand the change. It would be a tremendous adjustment, from an exciting and active independent life to a busy but family-centered one."

"And yet, Fran," I said, "I underscored in your book these words, 'The goal of a mature woman, whether married or single, is similar to the mature man's goal: to develop and use his energies and capabilities efficiently and productively.' And later you bring out the fact that self-giving and loving deeply are important in the life of any woman. If the single woman has had to be strong, as you brought out, she probably could make this shift with some grace."

"One thing bothers me, though," Fran said, "and that is that married people talk about how the Lord led them together, but no one talks about how the Lord led them to be single. It's always as though we are a minority and something odd, because there's something wrong if you aren't married. It's like all nice people are married, and all married people are nice. I believe that God has meant for me to be single up to now. And being where God wants you to be at any one time is the secret of anyone's happiness."

In her book Fran had brought out the importance of acceptance, in contrast to sublimation or a passive resignation. "Acceptance makes life positive, exciting, and fulfilling," she had said. "Completeness comes only with self-acceptance and self-awareness, and this is an ongoing search."

An ongoing search, for Fran or for me.

For, as Fran so aptly put it, "Happiness, this kind of maturity, is a state of mind."

Dr. Peg Sankey: Women make good physicians. It's unfair to say mothering and practicing medicine are contradictory.

Two Doctors in the House

If you should call the second floor apartment of Dr. Peg Sankey some evening and ask, "Is there a doctor in the house?" you would likely get an affirmative response. And if you were lucky, you might be answered with the statement, "There are two doctors in the house tonight."

For Dr. Peg Sankey, a pathologist at Goshen (Indiana) General Hospital, is married to Dr. Craddock Duren, a specialist in internal medicine and Medical Director at the same hospital. Peg kept her professional name when she married for several reasons: changing her name would have involved adding to her diploma, changing her license, writing many letters of explanation, and causing a great deal of confusion when both doctors were practicing at the same hospital.

It was important to me that two doctors would be in the house when I rang the Duren doorbell, for I had met the doctors at a wedding and was intrigued by their joint plans and philosophies.

They told me that they had not met in medical school, however, for Peg, from Terre Haute, Indiana, had trained at Indianapolis, and Crad, from Milwaukee, Wisconsin, had trained at Madison.

"We met in Detroit during residency training, and if you recall the Detroit riots of 1967," Dr. Duren grinned, "you will know that it was only proper that gentlemen give aid and comfort to the ladies they might be close to. Actually, though, we met over the Bunsen burner. I had started a period of training in infectious diseases and Peg had to check blood cultures each morning in the Ford Hospital lab. Thus I met a young pathologist who was also serving her time in residency."

"Had you always wanted to be a doctor?" I asked Peg, who looks the part and has that determined air which seems to make a woman with serious intent.

"My father had been a schoolteacher for twenty-two years before he quit to farm. When I was about seven, I admired a cousin who was a nurse, and announced that that was what I would like to be. But my father said, 'No, you're going to be a doctor.' His idea then literally became mine, and we pursued it together. The other thing I would have liked to do was to go into foreign service of some kind. Crad and I think of combining our two interests — medical and foreign service — sometime."

"As a woman, did you experience any discrimination while you were in medical training?" I asked, remembering an article on the subject in a leading women's magazine.

"There were only nine women in a class of 161," Peg explained. "The main thing you had to prove was that you were literally 'one of the boys.' You may be feminine, that's not the problem, but you're going to work just as hard as they do, if not harder. For instance, I was assigned for a period to a Veterans Administration hospital, where all the patients were men except for a few OB patients.

"Although I never tried to be coy, the fellows thought that we had the advantage when being presented to an older staff person, who might respond to us in a softer manner than he would have to a male student. I don't think we consciously played on this, although each woman has certain mannerisms which are typically feminine. I think you got into greater trouble if you tried to act masculine, because then you really competed with the man, which sometimes made him angry. I remember one girl who boasted about her masculinity and created a great deal of hostility. On the other hand, another girl overplayed the feminine bit, saturating her handkerchief so heavily with perfume, that the fellows one morning surrounded her with cigar smoke, to dramatize their feelings."

I turned to Dr. Duren, to get his side of this issue. "How did you feel about the women in your classes?" I asked.

"As a rule, they got better grades and so they raised the grade level," he acknowledged. "Most of us, however, wanted girls to be girls. We wanted them to be feminine, and we liked it when they asked us to help them with something, such as moving a patient in a bed. We liked to open a door for a girl or help her with her coat. We tried to maintain the roles as much as possible. But there were some girls who resented this. They felt uncomfortable in a feminine, dependent role."

Peg did not think that she was discriminated against in choosing her specialty, but she pointed out that medical schools have quotas, and when they accept someone, they want to be sure that either a man or a woman is going to complete the training and go on into practice. Some fields, such as surgery, although open to women, are more demanding and therefore do not attract as many women as some other fields.

"How about discrimination in practice?" I wondered.

"I feel that you have to do a little more than the fellows to prove yourself. In Missouri, where I first practiced, sometimes a fellow would come into the lab and I would ask, 'Can I help you?' But he would look past me and ask for a male doctor to give the diagnosis. And often I would be given the lesser jobs. I don't have that trouble here in Goshen, because I am the only pathologist. Sometimes, when you're feeling particularly sensitive, these things do bother you a bit."

A typical day in the lives of the Drs. Duren and Sankey begins early enough to get them to their posts of duty around 7:00 a.m.

"We skip breakfast because it gives us more time to sleep," Crad injected. "We're still a young married couple, you know."

For the first hour or so Peg checks the laboratory

to see if things have been cleaned up from the previous day and checks the daily log sheets, as well as blood sugars and other tests. Sometimes there is an autopsy. At 10:00 there are pap smears, at 12:00 tissue slides from surgery of the previous day. And then there are reports to dictate, tours to make of the lab, and various tests to supervise — blood smears, abnormal hematology, bone marrow, etc. Working with Dr. Sankey are twelve full-time and nine part-time assistants, lab technicians, and office personnel. In her office Peg takes time to read professional journals, to see if there might be new tests which could be added or new ways of making tests.

Crad explained the importance of his wife's work from his own standpoint. "I have to be sure that someone is doing a quality control. Her responsibility is to make certain not only that the chemical test is most accurate, but also that results are prompt and personnel is conscientious. After all, patients are paying for both the actual test and for quality control."

When the two doctors arrive home at the end of a long day, there is still a house to keep, and I remembered, when I first met them, that Peg told me she does most of the cooking and Crad most of the cleaning.

"Peg and I can clean the house equally well," Crad said, "but she is a far better cook than I. She often does more than I do at home, however, because her hospital day is a little lighter than mine, and I am usually on call at night."

Days off are rare, and even part of the weekend

finds the couple on duty. Dr. Duren explains, "We work in a small hospital, and if you can't get a blood sugar or a cardiogram when needed, a patient may remain in the hospital an extra day, which at $40 or more a day is of importance."

What then do they do for recreation, if their time is so filled with their professional life? Peg likes reading, sewing, and cooking, particularly exotic foods — southern European, Asiatic, and Middle Eastern. And when they can get away, the couple likes to travel. Last year they visited Europe.

"Tiredness now is different from tiredness on the farm," Peg points out. "I used to drive the tractor ten hours a day. I was my father's best and most reliable farmhand. But there's a great deal of difference between physical and mental fatigue — with physical tiredness you can take a hot shower, sit down a few minutes, and be ready to go again. But mental fatigue doesn't go away easily, and you can awaken tired in the morning."

The Durens had been married two years when I interviewed them, the same length of time that they had been practicing physicians. I gathered enough courage and asked them if they planned to have a family.

Peg answered without reluctance. "Well, I don't think we have resolved the problem for sure. We are considering the possibility of adopting, if we feel we should have a family, since there are so many children already born who need a home."

"Would you keep on working full-time?"

Peg told me that she had had women friends who

seemed to have combined motherhood and their medical careers satisfactorily, taking out time to have their babies and then returning to work. One such mother went into residency in the morning hours and gave the afternoons to her family.

Crad interrupted here to point out that this plan would work only in a medical partnership arrangement.

Peg went on to explain her thinking. "I am a believer in the *quality* of parenthood, rather than the *quantity*, and knowing my personality, I would be a better mother if I were doing my other thing. I have heard the statement, 'Well, at least she stays at home and is a good mother.' But I don't think this is an adage which applies to everyone, that you are a bad mother because you go away or a good one because you stay home.

"And then there is the obligation to use my professional training. I think women make good physicians, and it is unfair to say that our ability to mother or to practice are mutually exclusive. Good day care centers are important, however.

"I thought at one time I would stay at home part time, but I learned I'm happier practicing. There's not that much to do at home. There have been changes in my thinking along the way, and I am sure there will be more changes five years from now."

Crad had a thought. "A good measure of the masculine role in white, middle-class America is how well a man does his work. Whether self-employed or not, if he does well, this boosts his masculine image. But if a girl advances in the business world, it doesn't add to her feminine image. She's supposed to do this by winning baking contests and being a well-groomed, gracious hostess."

This posed a problem in my mind. "Dr. Duren, if Peg would advance faster than you, would this threaten your masculine image?"

"I don't think so, because I am able to obtain enough recognition, acceptance, and attention in my professional role. Also, economically, I am able to make enough by myself to supply our needs."

"Money isn't your great aim in life, I take it."

"If it were, we would not be in Goshen, and I would be in some other specialty than internal medicine. Our satisfactions are from professional achievement. The best compliment anyone could give us is that we practice quality medicine."

Peg added, "Another compliment which I once received and hope I can retain is that I am not changed because of financial attainment. An old German lady once told me that she didn't think living in a fine house would change me. When I lived in rural areas, I thought Farm Bureau meetings, rural churches, etc., were trite, but I learned in Detroit that such social occasions as cocktail parties can be a lot more trite. People had not found any peace of mind; they were continually seeking. I gained so much from my rural background, that I guess it makes me hesitate to bring up children in a city environment."

Crad said, "You may notice that our apartment is pretty simple, a little sparse. We like to get along with as little furniture as possible, and live as simply as possible, so that if the Spirit moves us to leave, there won't be so much to pack. When you move every few years, you learn to keep things to a minimum."

I glanced around at the apartment, tastefully though simply furnished, and noticed that although it was most attractive, there was no clutter.

"Is it easy for two physicians to live together?" I wondered aloud.

"Well, you see, this is all we have ever been used to," Dr. Duren responded. "Before Peg and I were married we lived with other medical students, and we like having common intellectual interests and common understandings of problems."

"When I met you the first time, you told me you would not enjoy living with a woman who did not stimulate you intellectually," I remembered.

"Yes, we complement each other. While some people enjoy doing other than occupation-related activities in the evenings, we usually bring our work home with us, working on speeches, reading our own and one another's journals and books, etc."

Peg agreed. "I think one of the greatest advantages I have had was living with other girls in med school, and now being married to a physician. Nothing challenges me more than learning that somebody knows something that I don't. It's a good way of continuing my education."

"Are there also problems or adjustments peculiar to two doctors living in one house?" I asked, again getting personal.

Crad answered in a matter-of-fact way. The question didn't throw him. "One of the problems that we have had to face in our marriage is that each of us is a self-contained package. We were used to doing things on the spur of the moment. For instance, I would run to the barbershop, not because it was Friday, but because I had a cancellation. Now in marriage you have to start thinking about the other person. If we can't get one of our cars started in the morning, and we have to drive down together, that means we have to come home together, and there may be a certain amount of 'spinning our wheels' if one is ready to come home and the other is not. And also, we were used to living single, and having everything in order, so that if I can't find something in the house, I am sure Peg put it somewhere (although I may have misplaced it myself)."

Peg smiled. "I think this is one of the problems, not only of being two individuals, but of being married when you're older. It's the old story that it's the small things that irritate you, such as the squeezing of the proverbial toothpaste tube (fortunately, we agree on the same brand of toothpaste, without fluoride).

"On the other hand, being more mature when we married, I think we made a more solid marriage, and we don't handle our difficulties by jumping up and down or running home to Mother. We have told ourselves that there are few problems which cannot be decided on verbally."

"Then there is the problem of the girl having to switch roles when she comes home," Crad added. "At work Peg has to make multiple decisions, and she takes charge of things. At home she becomes more supportive. I want to be boss at home."

I looked at Peg, and noted that she did not appear oppressed.

"How do you like working in the same hospital?" I asked.

"We would actually prefer working in separate hospitals," Dr. Duren responded. Then he went on to explain, "We try to maintain separate identities at the hospital so that, for instance, a physician who tells Peg something in the morning will not get the idea that I will hear about it at lunch, or that I have the inside story on something related to one of his patients. For that reason, we don't go through the halls holding hands, and we sit separate at staff meetings. It is important that Peg is thought of as a separate person."

"I do go to Crad for advice sometimes," Peg inserted, "if someone asks me something about therapeutics, for example, or dosages, or something which I know little about. It saves looking it up."

"What do you think is an ideal marriage relationship, whether you are both physicians or not?"

Crad responded thoughtfully. "This separate identity works for us, but it would not work for everyone. Each person has his own needs, and some have very few needs. There are all sorts of ways of working things out. You have to know what you want in a marriage relationship, what the person you marry wants, and even though it is difficult, you have to be honest with one another. I wanted to know that I wasn't marrying a girl who expected to live in a mansion."

Peg told of a friend with "girl problems," who worried that someone might marry him for his professional status. "How do I know if they're interested in Paul B., or Paul B., MD?"

Peg had jokingly answered, "The easiest thing is to marry another professional."

Peg went on, "You have to be extremely careful about choosing your mate. It is important to discuss, before marriage, how much you expect to work, and make sure your husband doesn't mind. An understanding is absolutely essential."

Peg and Crad, in evaluating their lives, were glad that they were physicians and that they were married, although they agreed that marriage is not for everyone.

"I think that in America there is more pressure for a girl to marry than in Europe," Peg said, thinking of several European physician friends who chose not to marry. "If there is anything that makes me angry, it is to hear a mother say, 'When you grow up and get married,' taking it for granted that this is the only option for a female child. But being married has given me many valuable insights which I would not have were I not married."

As they think of their life together, the Durens consider that the period they are now enjoying, of obtaining their clinical experience, is an important and exciting chapter in their lives. What the future holds, they do not know at this point. Teaching in the field of medicine would appeal to them. And then there is foreign service, a lifelong interest which one might guess by the prominence of a large globe in their living room.

"If I had gone into the Peace Corps," Peg reminisces, "I would have been equally intrigued by being a farmer or a physician abroad, since I like both so well. I think of foreign service, not simply as helping others, but as a learning experience for myself. I feel people in other lands have as much to teach as we have to teach them."

The Durens are concerned that they never become complacent or indifferent to the suffering of others. "As in any profession, there are days when we become discouraged," Crad pointed out.

"And I miss the periods of solitude for meditation, sitting on a stump or beside a stream, which I had on the farm," Peg added. "I think I become more irritable or impatient without it."

It was then that Peg shared with me an ancient prayer which she has often read in the morning before making her hospital rounds. It is the prayer of Maimonides, written sometime between AD 1135 and 1204, and published in 1863 under the title, "Daily Prayer of a Physician Before Visiting a Sick Man."

I begin once more my daily work. Be Thou with me, Almighty Father of Mercy, in all my efforts to heal the sick. For without Thee, man is but a helpless creature. Grant that I may be filled with love for my art and for my fellowmen. May the thirst for gain and the desire for fame be far from my heart. For these are the enemies of pity and the ministers of hate. Grant that I may be able to devote myself, body and soul, to Thy children who suffer pain. Preserve my strength, that I may be able to restore the strength of the rich and the poor, the good and the bad, the friend and the foe. Let me see in the sufferer the man alone. When wiser men teach me, let me be humble to learn; for the mind of man is so puny, and the art of healing is so vast. But when fools are ready to advise me or to find fault with me, let me not listen to their folly. Let me be intent upon one thing, O Father of Mercy, to be always merciful to Thy suffering children.

May there never rise in me the notion that I know enough, but give me strength and leisure and zeal to enlarge my knowledge. Our work is great, and the mind of man presses forward forever. Thou hast chosen me in Thy grace, to watch over the life and death of Thy creature. I am about to fulfill my duties. Guide me in this immense work so that it may be of avail.

Sally Graber: Our many foster boys are part of the family. We treat them just like our own children. They feel wanted.

Mother to Troubled Teens

It had been a long time since I had rung Sally Graber's doorbell, and I could hardly wait. But as we approached, we were no longer on familiar ground. For the Grabers had sold their old farmplace in southeastern Iowa for a much larger one, a 500-acre estate replete with 200 acres of timber, a creek, ponds, fields for grazing, croplands, numerous farm buildings, three houses, and a mobile home. And to make it all even more impressive, we turned in at a stone entrance engraved with the word Greenhurst.

The Grabers had always lived on a farm, and their lands were a place of enchantment to children from nearby towns who were lucky enough to be invited for a day or a week at a time. Our own children had been among the fortunate ones, and an invitation to the Grabers' was a coveted passport to bliss. Now they had bought this larger place in order to extend hospitality to teenagers who were in trouble with the law.

"Our boys are gone for the afternoon," Sally explained, as she and her husband, Clarence, appeared to greet us and invite us into the cheerful, comfortably cluttered farm kitchen, the kind of kitchen that emits succulent odors and rewards hopeful appetites with homemade bread and cherry pie.

Of course, we admired the new place and the Grabers expressed their enthusiasm for their purchase. As we came in, their son Philip departed, headed for Indiana in his small plane, where he would visit his fiancée.

"Philip and his bride will be living in the mobile home," they explained, and Ruth Anne, and her husband, Jerry Eccles, in the smaller house. Dick a high school teacher and his family are already here, lending a hand when he can fit it into his schedule and during the summer months. We can hardly believe that our children are coming home to help us. It is wonderful."

As we visited around the kitchen table, Clarence took from the wall a framed map of Greenhurst, which he had discovered, after the purchase, in the upstairs room of the garage.

"This place belonged to a man named Warren Beckwith, way back in 1886," he told us, "and Beckwith was married to President Lincoln's granddaughter, Tod Lincoln's daughter. He was a well-to-do horse breeder, raising and selling horses and livestock, and President Lincoln often came to Mt. Pleasant to visit. Tod married Senator Harlan's daughter and owned a country house and a town house, close to the campus of Iowa Wesleyan College. The President liked to spend time with his grandchildren, but we don't know if he ever visited this place."

We laughed and conjectured that it was a possibility.

"How on earth did you ever find such a place?" we wondered.

"That is a story in itself," Sally told us. "Our other farm was 286 acres, and Dick thought we should be looking for a bigger one. Then a real estate man found out about this place and we looked at it. We thought it was fabulous, with its buildings — houses, shop, granary, and cattle sheds. But money was tight, and we found it hard to get a loan. Then one day a lady whom we had never met came to our door and said that she and her husband observed how Clarence had developed the other farm, improving the place and increasing the corn yield, and they would like to lend us the difference needed to purchase this one."

"How many children have you had in your home, over the years, counting foster children and juvenile delinquents?"

Sally thought a minute.

"Oh, around twenty, I would say. I counted sixteen who were fifteen or sixteen years old."

"How long did they stay with you?"

"There's no set time. One was here for four years, another two, and a handicapped boy who is now in a Goodwill school stayed with us over three years. He comes home every now and then to visit, as this is the only real home he has known. We have room for six, but this house is terribly inadequate, and we plan to move a larger house from town this year and remodel it.

"Dad and I hope that we can perhaps do this ten more years. He will be fifty-seven in March, and we have been blessed with reasonably good health. He has a good heart and good blood pressure."

"You have a good heart, that's for sure," I joked. But I didn't mean it as a joke. My children would never forget the good times they had had on the Graber farm. Clarence reminded us that our oldest daughter had broken her wrist at their place by falling off a pony, but even this did not dampen her enthusiasm.

Clarence pointed out some other assets of Greenhurst, as he showed us the map. "With lots of woods and a beautiful creek along the north end, it's a great place for canoeing and camping. Our son Dave [also a high school teacher] and his family like to come here for camping sometimes. And we found an old, old graveyard on the place. Perhaps we will be buried there ourselves."

"How do the boys you take in help with the farm operation?"

"Well," Clarence said, "we do some crop farming and have fifty-eight head of cattle, of which we milk something like thirty-five. The boys help with milking, and since we burn wood in the furnace, making wood is a big project. Then Philip is a certified mechanic and teaches them mechanics in the shop."

Clarence had spent as much time in the house as a farmer could readily spare, and my husband, Virgil, accompanied him out to the barn, while Sally and I went into the living room. As we settled on the couch, we could see some of the farm buildings through the window.

"How did you get started taking in juvenile delinquents?" I asked her.

"Earlier, you know, we took in younger foster children, just one or two at a time," she replied. "But one time, at a Farm Bureau meeting, a probation officer presented the need for foster homes for kids who are on probation, mostly teenagers. From the time that Clarence and I were married, we felt, well, as though we were here for a purpose, and our prayer was that we would not fail to take advantage of opportunities that came along. And our philosophy has solidified that if we really want to serve, God will flood us with opportunities. The great thing about God is that He'll put you somewhere where you enjoy being. And there's no place I'd rather be than at home.

"So we told the probation officer, that was in 1964, that we'd take these youngsters."

"You said you like to be at home. You were once a teacher, weren't you? Have you ever wished you could go back to teaching?"

Sally chuckled. "I was glad when my teacher's certificate ran out, so they'd no longer bother me about teaching. I just didn't want to go away and leave my children. I was twenty-seven when I got married, and I had sort of been here and there and everywhere all my life. I was raised in Kansas, and I was making my own way from the time I was seventeen, which isn't a bad thing, but my parents were very hard up and I wasn't able to be at home very much. Besides making my own living, I sent money home to my parents. I was so happy to have my own home that I wanted to be there.

"Being tall was always a problem to me, and I was teased about finding a man taller than myself. Clarence is a few inches shorter than I, but I came to the place where I did not think a man's worth was in his stature!

"And as for working, I have a really steady job, and it's as steady as any I could have anyplace. And I forego many things, because it is important that I am here. The minute the boys step in the door after school, usually I'm in the kitchen, they look for me and holler, 'Sally, are you home?'

"It's a great thing to know that you are doing something worthwhile, something that will help someone. We used to have a feeling of dissatisfaction, as though we weren't doing enough. Well, we were in a way, because we were bringing up a family, both of us were active in church, and I was teaching Sunday school and summer Bible school and directing a church chorus, and that sort of thing. But I had this inner compulsion that there was something else we could do."

"You mentioned your relationship with the boys who live here. Do they help you with the housework?"

"Yes, they take turns helping in the house for a week, and they like this. They're glad when their turn comes around, because they don't have to get up as early as for outside work and it isn't as hard, and we have fun. Since we started this, it has really helped our relationship. They get to know me better. I'm not just the one who gives the orders anymore. They find out I'm human. I can tease, and joke, and have a good time."

"What do they do to help?"

"Oh, they run the sweeper. clean the upstairs and the cellar, set the table at mealtime and help put on supper, clear the table, and stack things in the dishwasher." A look of sadness came across her face. "These boys come from difficult home situations. It isn't really their fault."

I thought this was a good time to draw Sally out on something which I had thought about, off and on, for quite a few years.

"Sally," I asked, "do you remember one time when you visited the church of which my husband was pastor, I was fluttering about, taking care of my children, and helping to produce a special worship service? You came to me and cautioned, 'Helen, while the children are little, you shouldn't try to do too many other things.'"

Sally laughed. "Did I say that? I hope I didn't hurt your feelings."

"Not at all. I needed to be reminded. But what was the context of your thinking? You had had a family longer than I had at the time."

"I believe that it is terribly important to make your little ones feel that you couldn't be happy if you didn't have them, that they are a most important ingredient to their mother's happiness. And we must help them feel their worth as individuals. The period the children are small and need their mother at home is such a short part of our lives. I have heard mothers complain that their teenage daughters won't do anything to help around the house. But I think if I'm home when they're little and let them help when they want to, it will carry over when they're older. I usually had two or three standing around the table when I was baking, playing with the dough and 'helping.'"

"I always felt you put the emphasis on the right things, that you weren't fussy about a lot of little details," I remembered.

Again Sally smiled. "Cleaning is anathema to me!"

"But it never got too bad, and you had time for people."

"Ruth Anne says, now that she is grown, she appreciates it that if Dad wanted someone to go along with him to make a fence, I would say, 'You can sweep the kitchen when you get back.' After all, it was a good opportunity to be with her dad."

"Sally," I pressed, "did you ever have a problem with role? Did you always feel fulfilled, as the saying goes?"

"We had our first five children pretty close together (five in seven years), and I'll admit there were times when I felt a little sorry for myself. But I really appreciated my children.

"When they were small, I helped with the milking, and we milked by hand. I would take a toddler along to the barn, so that he could watch the cows. We all helped a lot outside.

"After Esther came out of her baby stage, and everyone was old enough to help himself, Clarence and I thought this was the best time of our lives. We could take trips and go on picnics, and we did a lot of that sort of thing.

"Then they became teenagers, and oh, that was so exciting, to have the kids in high school. We had five teenagers one summer, and we thought this was the best time in raising a family. We worked on the farm together, went swimming, and if they were working on the back '80,' I'd take dinner out and we'd have a wiener roast or something. We were dairying and had chores, so we couldn't make long trips, but we'd take one-day jaunts to see historic places or to attend a Dairy Cattle Congress at Waterloo.

"Then the children got into college and began choosing their careers and futures, and we thought that that was the most exciting. And now there are grandchildren! We have come to the conclusion that every stage is the best."

Suddenly Sally gave a cry of joy. Ruth Anne and her husband, Jerry, had arrived for a visit. Although the young couple planned to fix up the little house on the farm in the spring, they were presently employed in Cedar Rapids, where Ruth Anne was an RN on a hospital ward.

I thought of the lawn wedding which my daughter had attended a few years before, when Ruth Anne and Jerry had repeated their vows under a rose arbor. Now Ruth Anne talked easily of her marriage and home, then excused herself to go to the kitchen and make chili soup for supper.

"Your children picked up your values," I observed. "It must be a real satisfaction."

"When our children come home, there are usually two or three conversations going at one time," she said. "When a child walks in, I drop everything and sit down and talk."

"You must have some remarkable insights into living with teens, having had six of your own and now taking in those other children."

"Our own children have had problems, too," she admitted, "and it's not been all a bed of roses. But we maintained their independence and respected it. You can't condemn a child and castigate him, telling him, 'You're a disgrace.' And since they are individuals in their own right, just because I think a certain way is no sign that they will think the same.

"I have a deep conviction that when our children have problems, and get into trouble, it is partly our fault. Some parents say to their kids, 'How could you treat us like that — do a thing like that to us? My feeling is that what they do to us is of little significance, that what's really important is helping them see what they're doing to themselves. And take a share in the responsibility. Kids need to learn, from little up, that they are responsible for what they do. But at the same time, if a teenager makes a mistake, we need to say to him, 'Now look here, you're my son or my daughter, and what's happened is regrettable, but just the same, I'm behind you and I want to help you. And I'm partly responsible too.'

"This is a new idea to them if you take part of the blame, and often they'll say, 'No, Mom, you're not really responsible.' "

"Have you other words of wisdom to pass on to parents, Sally?"

"One thing we have found to be very important, especially after taking in these troubled youngsters, is teaching simple obedience. I believe this can be done by consistently guiding children even when they are very young. And I believe this is essential to providing them with the security you hear so much about.

"When our children were little, this permissive doctrine was being promoted. Well, we had our first five quickly, and it didn't take us long to decide that permissiveness should be in small doses. Obedience was terribly important. It might mean the difference between life and death, or at least avoidance of accident or harm, if a child knew what it meant to come when you said 'come,' or not to do something when you said 'no.' Permissiveness could lead to chaos. Obedience taught in a loving way smoothed out a lot of rough spots.

"And, if children realize, as I said before, that they are *an important ingredient to their mother's happiness,* they will want to obey her. They'll want to be 'good' away from home."

"What would you do differently if you could raise your own children over again?" I asked.

"Well, I certainly wouldn't want to live my life over again — I might do it worse than I did! I've had a pretty good life, you know. But I would take more advantage of opportunities to talk about God, and with Him, with my children. And I would certainly try to have more patience, especially when

they're small. I would give God more credit for answered prayers, making sure the children knew about
it. Well. . . ."

We were soon following the beckoning aroma of
chili into the kitchen, where we were joined around
the ample table by Clarence and Virgil, son Dick and
his wife, Nancy, and their two babies, and Ruth Anne
and her husband, Jerry.

And while we talked, joked, and reminisced, we
learned more about the boys who normally ate at
the table. Yes, they did accompany the Grabers to
church services.

"We couldn't have it any other way," Sally told
us. "If the boys rebel and say that they want their
freedom to stay home, we tell them we want our
freedom to go to church and they could not be left
at home unsupervised. Then we have family prayers
each morning before school."

Actually, two of the boys have joined the church of
which the Grabers are members, and one has been
vice-president of the youth group and an usher in
the church. The boys participate in Youth for Christ
activities, which is where they were during our visit.

But the going is not always smooth. The Grabers
described times when the fellows became dissatisfied
and bored, sick of the daily routine (just as their own
children had been at times). However, with their
emotional problems, crises could become severe. Two
had recently run away and had to be reclaimed at
the police station. Threats of violence, revenge, or
suicide were not uncommon, and the Grabers testified
to freedom from anxiety, special grace not their own,

and an ability to "keep on loving those boys in a way we never could in our own strength."

Philip, 24, had given three years in Voluntary Service in a home for delinquent boys in Indiana, and was trained in mechanics at LeTourneau. He had already proved a valuable asset in the work and hoped, after his marriage, to continue to teach mechanics, perhaps starting a business repairing wrecked cars.

"Dad and I are often either too easy or unreasonable with the boys," Sally said. "Philip relates well."

Some incidents they described were not major crises. They sounded familiar to parents of any teens.

"I have a policy here that when they don't make their bed or pick up their things, they get fined a dollar," Sally related. But one boy, after three days of refusing to make his bed, announced soberly, "I just want you to know, Sally, that fining isn't going to do me any good."

"Well, Mike, if you wanted to teach a boy something, how would you go about it?" Sally had asked, to which he had answered, "That's your problem, not mine." And he had continued to refuse to cooperate.

Finally Sally pinned a sign on Mike's bed: "Fined $4.00. What do you want? A messy bed and no money to spend? The choice is yours."

The bed was made the next day.

But, although discipline is resented at the moment, letters from the boys indicate their appreciation of the Graber home. One, from a fellow who ran away, read, "Why didn't you kick me in the rear when I didn't behave? If I'd stayed there, I might have learned something. Could you take me back?"

"The boys live right here with us," they told us. "They're our family, and we treat them just like our own children. And even if they hate this place, in spite of themselves they begin to feel part of us."

As our table talk went on, we touched on a variety of subjects in an animated conversation reminiscent of bygone times: their youngest daughter, Barb, who would be a foreign exchange student next year, ecology, young people and the church, family relationships, dorm living at college, and plans for developing the farm. Son-in-law Jerry had ideas for a trailer court. All the men talked of stocking the pond, crop fishing, planting nut trees in the orchard. One had a feeling of frontiersman adventure as they talked.

And I had another feeling, as I looked around the table at the faces of children and grandchildren of a twentieth-century virtuous woman. I saw that children do yet rise up and call a mother blessed.

Ruth Anne expressed it when she remembered how her mother had assured her that cookies were family property and that taking one was not stealing.

"Now how did you know then, Mom," she asked, "that you shouldn't give a child a guilt complex?"

I saw it in the respect that Dick and his spouse showed to a grandmother who delighted in their little ones but did not spoil them.

And I heard it when Sally read portions of a letter from daughter Esther, teaching school in New York City and about to be married. After describing the simple wedding which the couple would have, Esther wrote, "We want it to be a joyful and God-with-us occasion."

If Esther's wedding was a sample of the daily life at Greenhurst, it would indeed be joyful and God would be there.

Doris Lehman: I have always tried to make sure that the family is not suffering from my own personal involvements.

Sifter of Priorities

It was about time that I visited Doris Lehman in her "natural habitat," I thought, as I rang the doorbell of her pleasant two-level suburban home on Yellow Creek, in Elkhart, Indiana. Somehow it seemed that our only opportunities for visiting occurred during intermission at some large women's meeting. But since Doris and I have a lot of ideas in common, we are usually able to compress a fair amount of verbal exchange in a few minutes' time.

I knew that Doris had her own ideas about the role of Christian women. She headed up the national women's organization of the Mennonite Church and for the six previous years had chaired the district chapter. She was one of the first women on one particular committee of her denominational mission board. She was often called on as a retreat speaker and spoke or gave homemaking demonstrations to numerous women's groups around the country. And she led a community Bible study, for which she had great enthusiasm.

But I knew that Doris could not live with her conscience if she neglected her family, which was composed of her husband, David, an orthodontist, and six children, ranging in age from seven to seventeen. To put it in her own words, Doris "struggles with priorities."

After Doris invited me in, we strolled over to the large picture window beside the dining room table and looked down on the thorn-apple tree where the Lehmans watch their bird friends while both they and the birds eat their dinner. Beyond was a patch of woods between us and Yellow Creek. Doris told me that the family has a rope swing which glides right out over the creek, a joy to the children and their friends.

"Doris, a long time ago I met you at a meeting, where we always seem to get together, and you told me that you really battled with the problem of how many church and community responsibilities you could take on. Your children were quite a bit younger then."

"Yes," she responded, "when I accepted my first major job with women's work, a neighbor said, 'How can she do that with all those little children?' Well, I cared about 'all those little children' myself. And this was a challenge to serious thinking about priorities."

"Are you still at it?"

She dimpled. "I sure am. I have always tried to make sure that the family was not suffering from my own personal involvements. It seems to me that for any Christian woman the home and family are her first responsibility, and if we don't meet the emotional needs of our children, no one else will. And now I think I struggle more, because with the children older they are involved in so many activities themselves. It pulls at me in a new way. I feel I should have fewer involvements in their high school years, just before they leave home. These years there is a constant hum of activity."

"Such as?"

"Well, I feel like Mrs. Basketball right now because I have a couple of cheerleaders, one basketball player on the high school team, and two girls on the junior high team. We don't attend all the games, but we enjoy sports and find a change of pace to be good; so we do attend quite a few of them."

"It takes a lot out of you emotionally to keep up with all their interests, doesn't it?" I empathized.

"That is why this fall, in sifting my priorities, I chose not to accept any assignments to speak at retreats, although I enjoy retreats. It made for a much saner fall and winter."

I knew that a family and service had never been mutually exclusive in the lives of Doris and David Lehman, although the combination occasioned Doris' much thinking about choices. She gave me a run-down on the history of their family since the first days of their marriage, when Dave was still a student in a dental school in Indianapolis. During the first years of their sojourn in that city, David had obtained his degree and Doris had applied her home economics training to a position as Home Demonstration Agent.

"That was an exciting kind of job," she said in her vivacious way. "I specialized in food demonstrations, such as economy meals, desserts, and so on, but I also did demonstrations on subjects like lampshade covering, drapery-making, crafts, textile painting, whatever the ladies in the Home Ec clubs requested. I did a lot of work at 4-H clubs and at county fairs, and gave demonstrations on a local television station."

While they were still living in Indianapolis, David accepted a two-year position at a mental screening hospital and the couple lived in a huge, three-story center for fellows living in the city and engaged in alternative service (in lieu of military service). As hostess, Doris cooked for twenty people and the Lehmans helped arrange worship services for a couple hundred boys scattered around the city.

Since David went to graduate school for two more years' training in orthodontia, the Lehmans lived in Indianapolis a total of seven years, and had a family of three small children when they left for a two-year assignment as dentist for a rural town in Puerto Rico. Doris told me that her time there was pretty well occupied with her children, although she also worked on her Spanish, taught a class in crafts in a church-related school, and had served as a teacher in summer Bible school.

"Did you have any problem with conflicting interests while you were doing all that?" I probed.

"Not really," she said. "We did everything together. The whole family enjoyed Puerto Rico, and it was a good experience. It was really no sacrifice for our preschoolers and we were delighted recently to go back and visit as a family.

I was looking for some cues which Doris had picked up in her search for family cohesiveness, and thought I had found one here in her reference to togetherness. I asked her to tell me more about including the family in the broader interests she and Dave espoused.

"We're in God's work together, and we use our home together," she said. "I remember, when I was on the slate for national president of the Women's Missionary and Service Commission, asking the children how they felt about it. Should I accept if I were voted in? The immediate reaction of one of the girls was, 'Mother, would you be bringing home interesting guests?' She remembered that Elisabeth Elliott had been a guest in our home and that there had been other interesting events resulting from my church assignments. Through the years our children have felt a part of it. There are things which the family likes to do cooperatively, such as entertaining. Having guests is a good learning experience because the children feel motivated to help and learn the correct ways of doing things."

Of course, there was someone whose approval might be more crucial, and I was eager to quiz Doris about him. I knew that David had his own involvements in church and community, and an agenda of his own, outside his professional career.

I asked about David's activities, and Doris told me that he had just been voted as Elkhart Layman of the Year for his work with the Leighton Ford Evangelistic Crusade, that he was president of the high school PTO, president of the Alumni Association of his alma mater, and active in the district mission board of his church.

"Our main problem is meshing our schedules," Doris pointed out. "We find it helpful to have an appointment book lying beside the telephone, where we both record our appointments. We have a policy to be careful not to both be involved in something big at the same time, that is, unless we are going somewhere together. It can be quite a point of pressure if we both have major projects going simultaneously."

"How does Dave feel about your projects?"

"I feel that to make things run smoothly and to make our home and marriage work, I can't be involved in things where I don't have my husband's support. But over the years Dave has been very, very supportive. I think he knows that being involved in women's work has done something for me. Even though he often had to take care of the children so that I could go, he's done this very generously."

Doris went on to say that she always gets David's reaction before she takes on a major assignment, such as a retreat.

"At one point a few years ago Dave felt that a good guide was for me to limit myself to one special project a month, and I thought this was helpful. That was about all I could handle with the routine when the children were small. Down through the

118

years we've adjusted that a bit, but I still think it's a pretty good plan."

I have a natural curiosity when it comes to how my friends order their everyday existences, and I wanted to know how a home economist such as Doris planned her workaday week. She told me that cleaning wasn't her greatest joy and that it helped her with her other activities if she scheduled cleaning jobs for Monday and Friday.

And, although she could afford to hire a certain amount of help, she would not do much of this because she wanted her children to be responsible for part of the work load. Her children were expected to clean their own bedrooms and to keep the basement family room, where they entertained their friends, in good condition. Each child had his night to do dishes during the week, and the girls helped with the cooking and baking, in addition to doing their own mending and some of their ironing. They also liked to sew and had learned much of this on their own initiative. The boys in the family were more likely to be assigned lawn work and related tasks.

"We do a lot of canning and freezing in the summer," Doris said, "and this is a family project. Everyone helps pick blueberries, strawberries, cherries, and other fruit and to put them away."

"They do all this cheerfully?" I asked, becoming uncomfortable with the thought that some families might be more successful in motivating than our own.

She laughed. "No children in my acquaintance enjoy work so much that they never complain. We have schedule conflicts since the children are older."

"If you do all your cleaning on Monday and Friday, how do you spend the rest of the week?" I inquired. I knew one of Doris' greatest interests was Bible study, and she told me that she was in the process of reading the Bible through consecutively and enjoyed doing that in the quiet hours of the morning, after the children had gone to school. And one afternoon a week she was joined by nine neighbors from within a block of her house, all women who felt a need for a meaningful Bible study.

"What do you study, and how do you go about it?" I wanted to know, and she told me that together they had read the books of Philippians and James in the New Testament and were now studying the Psalms.

"We react to a passage on paper, either paraphrasing it, stating our feelings about it, or writing down practical problems which it brings to our minds. If it is a story passage, I like to imagine myself as one of the characters, and think how I would have felt, for instance, if I had been in that boat with Jesus. I like to go to the Scriptures, especially with the modern versions that are available, without too many other helps.

"Really, I'm impressed with how these small sharing groups have helped women verbalize their faith in delightful ways."

Of course, having accepted responsibilities in the nationwide church as well as her own congregation Doris had plenty to keep her busy. She told of her concern, as chairman of her local women's group, to involve all the women in outreach and to encour-

120

age them to use their particular gifts in the ministry of the church. "Here is someone who visits well. She takes a little welcoming gift from the church to newcomers in the community. Another woman is our ecology secretary; she is gifted in stimulating projects which help us all to save."

"All of this takes a lot of time, doesn't it?"

"Yes, but as I give myself to correspondence, planning talks, committee work, and so on, I feel that, with my particular gifts, this is a valid way for me to spend my time right now. If we say we don't have time, we usually mean that we don't care to spend it in a certain way."

"I have a lot more questions to ask you about your 'Mary' activities in the work of the church, Doris," I said, "but first of all I'd like to pursue your 'Martha' life a bit more. I have a feeling that, as a former home demonstration agent, you would have some secrets to pass on to the rest of us."

My visit with Doris Lehman was often punctuated with a rippling and merry laugh, and she gave forth with one such, as she said, "Really, I'm not all that wise. But we have such good tools these days, and I'm blessed with good health. But I'm not a perfectionist, and sometimes the floor could use sweeping on days I don't take time for it. Knowing that I'll get around to it on Friday, we can stand it for a little while.

"But one thing I think my training in home economics has taught me is the importance of keeping some sense of order. If I don't let my work pile up, it is much easier. I try to do today's work today, plus a little extra. Even if it's just a clean closet, for instance, that tells of my special effort for that day, I know that I did something today that will not need to be done tomorrow.

"Then, too, I don't function well in a cluttered environment. Life for me, even physically, functions better and is more beautiful uncluttered. Every morning when the children leave I try to put things in order for the day. Sometimes I run off at 8:30 and don't get it done, but when it works, it's satisfying."

"Do your children put away their own things, such as wraps and school books?"

"Well, we're working at it, but we're like everyone else. One thing that I have had a problem with and keep working at along the line of priorities," she went on, "is to simplify. I tend to clutter my life maybe more than I clutter my house. I read once that 'beauty blooms when framed in space.' That really hit me because I feel that many times I try to do too many things. I am attempting to think of ways to simplify, not to the point of excluding important things, but rather to frame important things in space. Sometimes I have to choose not to do something that would have been valid, but would have cluttered my schedule. I have a long way to go in this.

"Another thing, I believe in living one day at a time, and not cluttering the day with worry about what I didn't get done yesterday or worry about the future. I think that giving each day to God and living in that day keeps life uncluttered for me."

"You mentioned your good health a while ago. What is your philosophy on staying physically fit? By the way, is your age a secret?"

It wasn't. Doris told me that she was forty-three, and then went on to say, "Both Dave and I believe in good nutrition. He says that what's good for your teeth is good for your body, and both of us give careful attention to diet. We have never excused our children from eating something simply because they say they don't like it. We have a garden and have preserved a lot of vegetables, and we discourage sweets between meals. I think it has paid off because the children have had almost no tooth decay in fifteen years."

"That is a record, even for a dentist's family," I said. "What do you do for exercise?"

Doris told me that she had earlier adhered to an exercise regimen, but found it tiresome to do the exercises alone. "But I get some exercise since I have no telephone downstairs where I often work, and I bound upstairs and try to answer the phone on the third ring. And then all of our family enjoys snow skiing. Dave has chosen this as a sport for himself, rather than something he would do alone. We're thankful for this."

She chuckled. "When our youngest graduates from the beginning slopes where I expect to stay, maybe I'll have to retire to the lodge with my knitting, but at least for the present I'm on the slopes with the rest of them."

"What do you do as a family in the summer?"

"A week of family camp, when we enjoy picnics and water sports together. And I like to surprise them and hit a ball, too. We do a lot of playing together," she said.

While she was still on the subject of her family, Doris began a psalm of thanksgiving.

"I tell you, life has been richer than I ever could have dreamed it would be. God has blessed us with so much of meaning and purpose, that I feel we are terribly responsible in light of it all. The children have given us a lot of happiness. Their struggle for independence is already becoming obvious, but we have enjoyed their growing up. It seems to me that if I live with the philosophy that life right now is as good as it ever has been or ever will be, life really has meaning."

"Doris," I observed, "you sound pretty liberated to me. Do you have a definition of liberation?"

Obviously, she had thought this one through before I asked it, for her response was immediate.

"I think that being liberated is being free to pursue the interests to which I feel called as a Christian and a woman. And this involves those things which I choose to do because I care about other people. I feel liberated doing my housework because this is for people I love. Housework doesn't make me feel bound because I choose to do it."

I liked Doris' definition, and I knew that her liberated caring about people carried over to her work in the church.

"In your work on the Overseas Missions Committee of the church, what contribution do you feel you make as a woman?" I wondered.

"I have really enjoyed this committee, and I feel I have something to contribute," she answered, "particularly in relation to problems of women in missions. I think women feel less inhibited in meeting with the Overseas Committee if there are women sitting there and asking questions from their own orientation."

"How would you say your understandings and concerns differ from those of the men on the committee?"

"Perhaps women have a world concern different from men. Men tend to be more calculating and involved in the financial detail of things, while I find myself wanting to say, 'Well, if it's valid, we'll find a way to do it,' and move on in the inspiration of it.

"I think I feel inclined to look at questions that come up from more of a *personal* point of view. I ask, for instance, 'How did this affect the way you *felt* about it?' Maybe approaching a question less objectively, maybe with more intuition, with more sense of my own feeling about it. Sometimes I'll say, 'Somehow I just can't feel right about this.

"Although I feel there is a lot of variety in the way men approach a question, more often women would approach it from this point of view, with more feeling and sensitivity."

"You do see a difference, then, in the way men and women approach a problem?"

"Yes, I think we approach life a bit differently, and that our roles are influenced by differences in our physical, emotional, and psychological makeup. I would not feel comfortable as chairman of a committee made up predominantly of men (maybe this is a hang-up) even though I am aggressive in women's groups. Yet, I do feel very well accepted."

"What do you think about women's work in the church? Should we continue to have an organization just for women, apart from the rest of the work of the church?"

Maybe this was odd to ask a woman who heads such an organization. But Doris was not defensive.

"Perhaps a women's organization is not as necessary as in years gone by, when there were few ways for women to express themselves. Women's work is much more a part of the total now. We are encouraging women to accept positions on boards and committees, to participate in the work of the church on all levels. But we are still keeping a WMSC because not all women care to give their gifts in the same way, and there will always be some things that women can do better, some things of service and productivity that women love to do in their homes and with each other. We want to continue to provide opportunities to serve one another and to reach out into the community."

"Come to think of it," I said, "it would be a little hard to knit bandages and knot comforters during the Sunday morning worship service. Why did you change the name of the organization from Women's Missionary and Service *Auxiliary* to *Commission?*"

"Well, I have no objection to being a member of a dental auxiliary," she replied, "because I'm not a dentist. But some of us didn't think it was appropriate to be an auxiliary of a church. That's where we liberationists rebelled! I am a Christian along with my

126

husband, and we're in the church together."

It was 3:00 p.m. and the door opened unceremoniously. One by one Ann, 17 and a high school senior, Margaret Sue, 14 and an eighth-grader, Jane, 13 and in the seventh grade, Mary, 10 and a fifth grader, and seven-year-old Joey drifted in, came over to be introduced to their mother's guest, and went about their evening activities. Only 16-year-old David, Jr., practicing basketball, did not appear while I was there.

With each child's appearance Doris took time to hear his comments on the day, answer questions, and make comments of her own. One daughter had a problem. What should she do about two events being scheduled for the same time that night?

"They have conflicting priorities, too?" I noted, and Doris assured me that the problem was not confined to the later years.

"Actually," she told me, when no one was asking for her attention, "I see life as a daily adventure, with so much of the unexpected, of risk-taking, of discovery in our relationship with God. And there have been those little miracles, household help offered when I was in a dilemma, a word of telephoned counsel when I was depressed because I felt I had failed in delegating responsibility, a word of affirmation at the right moment."

I had to think of Doris' definition of the liberated woman — someone free to do the will of God, as she felt called to do it. Someone who could choose her priorities. For a woman in this frame of mind, how could life help being an adventure?

127

Betty Cheen: I don't think we should ask the state to care for our parents if we are able to do it.

Love to the Children's Children

To ring Betty Gheen's doorbell, I drove past the Civil War monument and restored colonial homes of Leesburg, Virginia, took a wooded road west through the rolling foothills of the Blue Ridge, passed numerous estates owned by well-known Americans, and turned into a long driveway of an old-fashioned farmhouse.

Grandmother Gheen was, as usual, sitting on the porch.

My visit climaxed a warm acquaintance with Betty of almost thirty years. Once before I had had the privilege of visiting her home, but most of our friendship during our married years had been kept alive through letters.

Betty's quarter century of married life had been distinguished by the fact that, during the entire period, three generations had dwelled happily under one roof, enriching one another and lending a security extolled by sociologists but seldom worked out so ideally. Of course, Betty would be the first to admit that things did not always go smoothly. But nevertheless not only Grandmother Gheen, her husband Ralph's 90-year-old mother, lived with the family, but Ralph's father and an older aunt of Betty's had been part of the household until they died.

I had found a ride to Betty's home with friends who were going farther south. As Betty hurried out to meet us and to usher me into her homey kitchen, I noted that, save for the splashes of gray that seem a trademark of our particular age-group, Betty was the same girl I had known all those years before, her earnest manner frequently broken by laughter.

Betty and I have always viewed our friendship with a bit of awe, both because of the way we got acquainted, and the depth and longevity of our encounter. Both sixteen years of age and just out of high school (we were born the same week), we had landed in the same government typing pool in wartime Washington. Thereafter we had lunched together for at least three years, discussing our families, ideas, boyfriends, and books we chose to read together. Once we had tried an evening job in a department store during Christmas just for the fun of it, and I had stayed overnight with Betty.

Now as we sat down in the kitchen for a glass of iced tea and some reminiscing, Betty and I were joined by Grandmother Gheen and blond, 12-year-old Linda, who was in and out with her pets, a bird's nest she had found, and later her neighbor friend, Heather.

Grandmother remembered well my previous visit to Leesburg, and had always shared in my letters to Betty, so we already felt pretty well acquainted. As Betty shaped some dinner rolls, we talked, and I marveled at Grandmother's phenomenal memory. Betty told me later that although, like many other older persons, Grandma sometimes forgot more recent events, her memory of the old days was sharp and detailed.

Grandmother Gheen had married in 1896 at sixteen and was almost nineteen when her first baby was born. She chuckled at her ignorance of housekeeping; her first meal had no seasoning at all — that had sent her to older friends for counsel and help. These neighbors had generously taught her principles of cooking, keeping house, and what was involved in having a baby. She often quoted Aunt Jennie, a former slave, who offered her sage advice and reminded her that just having a baby did not make a woman a mother. "Modern women couldn't take what we did then," she thought aloud. "My mother had nine children and she worked hard."

Grandma went on to tell about her own children, five strong boys and one little girl who had died at the age of six. She had never gotten over the disappointment of losing her only girl-child. She expressed appreciation for her daughters-in-law. "All of them are fine women, hardworking, industrious, and good to me," she said.

Betty paused in her breadmaking. "We're the lucky ones," she responded. "Grandmother, tell Helen about the blizzard of 1898."

When Grandma, yet a teenager, was expecting her first child the memorable storm had covered her world with its freezing blanket of snow and extreme cold that penetrated walls. Alone some of the time, she had to keep on her long, warm winter coat to ward it off and had kept a good fire going in the fireplace. But still canned goods in the room with her had frozen.

We discussed other things, hopping from subject to subject and decade to decade. When we talked about storms, Grandmother recalled hearing that animals attract lightning. Betty didn't think so. And Grandmother described why she had never been afraid of electrical storms. "I still remember," she told us, "that when I was little, my mother called us children together during a storm and said, 'Now children, we are going to watch God's power.' I was never afraid after that."

When Ralph, tall and soft-spoken, came in from his job at the Leesburg Post Office, I asked him if he still played his guitar, for I remembered that is how he and Betty had got together in the first place. Yes, he still played country music in a Saturday night group called "The Potomac Valley Boys," and they had made a record. But the children did most of the music-making at their house now, and Betty declared that the rest of the family had gotten so good, "I can't keep up with them anymore."

Interestingly enough, Barbara, who was 21, a college senior, and working at her summer job in the bank when I arrived, had also gotten acquainted with her friend Eddie through music. They played and sang in a religious folk music group known as the '98'ers,' giving their programs of song and testimony in church and at Youth for Christ rallies. Jimmy, Betty's 19-year-old son, was a member of the same group and was on a musical tour in the Midwest during my visit. He played the guitar, the baritone, and the bass fiddle, and had gone to computer school during the past year.

As we sat around the supper table Barbara, now home from work, complimented her Grandmother on her new apron, which she was wearing for the first time since her birthday. Linda hinted strongly that her father should get busy and "break" the two horses the family owned so that she could ride them. Barbara told of the old horse she had enjoyed when younger, sometimes riding and reading a good book at the same time.

As the relaxed evening wore on, Eddie arrived and was persuaded to play us a tune. Betty and I talked as we sat on the porch and watched Linda and a neighbor play a game of badminton on the spacious front lawn, and Ralph filled me in on the historical significance of the area and some of the interesting personages who lived in or near Leesburg. Arthur Godfrey, for one, lived "just over the hill as the crow flies," and had owned his farm in Loudoun County for many years. Oak Hill, home of President James Monroe, is a few miles out of Leesburg, and General George Marshall's home is just on the outskirts of town.

They showed me a newspaper clipping, with a picture of Ralph taken when he had completed twenty-five years at the post office. The clipping said that he had had a full week and a busy month in February of 1946, having been discharged from the Armed Services on February 12, married on February 14, and starting work at the post office on February 18.

But it was not until the next morning that Betty told me the story of their marriage and the contribution that three generations had made to one another over the years. We were sitting in Jimmy's room, and Grandmother was busy in hers.

Betty and Ralph had not lived in an apartment long until they were searching out a place in the country. And when they found a small farm of sixteen acres, large enough for a garden, a few cows and horses, and some chickens, it seemed natural for Ralph's parents to join them, as their other sons all lived in town.

By this time Granddaddy was 72 and still active, although he was no longer able to farm on his own. There was plenty to keep him busy, however, on his son's acreage, and Ralph, working all day at the post office, was grateful. Granddaddy cleared much of the land, which was grown up with brush when the Gheens purchased it. No one needed to tell him how to care for a garden, or livestock, or the buildings, for this had been his world.

"He was a little man," Betty told me, "though you wouldn't know it to look at Ralph. But he worked fast, and there was never a weed in his garden."

Little Jimmy followed his granddaddy around and was his constant companion, riding in a wheelbarrow or eating apples as the old man peeled them for him.

134

"That's beautiful," I said to Betty, as she described Jimmy's memories of his grandfather.

"And how did Grandmother fit into your household? Did you have a system of dividing up the work?" I asked.

"We didn't really work it out. Grandmother would just pitch right in, diapering the babies or working in the kitchen. She's always been one of the family, you know. She saw what needed to be done, and did it. And they knew they were helping and were needed. There was always a lot to be done."

"But she let you be the wife of the house?"

"Oh, yes. She never offered a word of advice, so far as our marriage is concerned. And she just loved the children and of course wouldn't let them get hurt or anything, but as far as bossing them is concerned she never did that. That is where she's unusual, I think."

We laughed as we recalled the story Grandmother had told about Jimmy the day before.

"Jimmy is so cute," she had said.

Betty had teased, "A cute six-foot-four?"

But Grandmother was remembering the time Jimmy, as a tiny lad, had got caught in the briar patch. And she told her other favorite stories about the children — Barbara's prayer of thanksgiving when Jimmy was born, the time four-year-old Barbara had blamed two-year-old Jimmy for their sneaking off to the neighbors without permission. And the time little Barbara, unable to find more strawberries in the patch, had come home with her pail filled with shiny stones.

"There are certain things they remember the best," Betty said. "We were so lucky, because both Grandmother and Granddaddy had such good dispositions. A lot of times older people aren't well, and it isn't their fault, but little children get on their nerves. This was never the case with Ralph's parents. Granddaddy lived nine years after he moved here. All his sons and their wives were crazy about him, and up until two years ago Grandmother made the rounds spring and fall, spending a week or two with each of her other children. They love having her, but it is too hard for her to move around now. She needs her own room, where she can find her medicines and other things."

"That reminds me of something that Grandmother said to me yesterday," I remembered. "She said, 'I'm just an old hen who likes to roost in the same place every night.'"

Betty added, "Or sometimes she'll say, 'I like to climb up on the same pole.' Even if older people are shuffled about from one child to another, I think they need the security of having one place that can be their own. Did you look at Grandmother's room? It is interesting, because she collects pictures of animals, birds, and flowers, as well as her many photographs. She also keeps clippings of people and places she has known over the years. Barbara likes to go through her clippings sometimes. She likes old things.

"I think it's important that older people have a room where they can do as they please. It may not look as neat, and it may not be in keeping with the rest of your house, but their own things, such as Grandmother's rocker and her sewing machine, are important to them. I have a much better bed stored in the attic, but Grandmother prefers her old iron one."

"And where did your Aunt Blanche fit into this picture?" I could still remember Betty's letters when all three of the older generation were with her family at the same time.

"Aunt Blanche had taken me when I was three years old because my mother was sick and could not take care of all of us children," Betty explained. "She loved children and was not able to have any of her own, so she kept me during my school years, and was a second mother to me, After her husband died, she worked a few years in Leesburg, but when because of high blood pressure she was no longer able to work, we invited her to live with us. She was with us eight years, but was ill much of the time."

"Then how did she get along with Ralph's parents? Was there any feeling of competition?"

Betty could not remember that there was. "She and Grandmother kept each other company and got along well," she said. "They soon discovered that they had known some of the same people in their youth, and they liked to visit. And then, when Aunt Blanche could no longer work, Grandmother helped to wait on her. Grandmother also took care of Granddaddy before he died.

"I think that is the most important thing — to feel needed. No one likes to think that they're of no use to people. And Aunt Blanche was like the grandparents, in that children didn't get on her nerves. She loved little babies, and when Linda was born, it was the first time she had lived in a house with a new baby. She thought Linda was a lump of gold!"

I asked the inevitable: "Did those older people spoil your children?"

Again, Betty smiled. "They made a fuss over them, but they didn't spoil them, really. And they never did anything behind our backs. I think that would be really bad, if the older people would take up for the children when you disciplined them. One thing, though, when you have grandparents around, you find yourself bending over backwards not to discipline too harshly in front of them, because it hurts the grandparents more than it does the child! In that way they could get a bit spoiled.

"But when Linda was born, everyone had fun with her. Our other children were eight and ten years old, and Barbara loved carrying her around. As far as Grandmother and Aunt Blanche were concerned, she was the perfect baby. Grandmother says that every time she gets a new grandchild or great-grandchild (and she is still having them), it renews her life."

"You know, Betty, I observed, "you have what they call an extended family. Now I know you didn't sit down and read a sociology book which told of the advantages of this kind of family unit over the smaller nuclear family, but you just did it. And I see a real stability in it for your children."

Betty told me that the family was even more extended than I saw on this visit, since their home was frequently a gathering place for the entire Gheen clan. When Ralph's family gathered for a picnic on the lawn and a visit with their mother, there were about fifty children and grandchildren present, she told me. Besides that, Grandmother's oldest son, now retired, came out weekly to visit her, and as long as she was able she accompanied her children to church services.

"From your twenty-five years of experience, Betty, what would you say are the greatest needs of older persons?" I asked.

"There are just two things that I can think of," she answered. "First, as I said before, to know that they are needed and have something worthwhile to do. And second, to feel that people care about them, especially their children."

On the first point, Betty told the contribution Grandmother was still able to make around the house — how she kept everything mended, darned the socks, and always washed the dishes. "We wouldn't think of getting a dishwasher and taking her job away from her," Betty mentioned. "And she likes working with fruits and vegetables from the garden." I was to see that demonstrated that very day, as Grandmother, Betty, and I shelled peas and talked.

As to people taking time for her, Betty told me that Grandmother's spirits could drop and she could become despondent if no one came to see her for a while. Fortunately, her children did come often, and neighbors dropped in from time to time to listen to her reminisce and bring her little gifts, such as a jar of jelly or a few flowers. So much did she prize small tokens of love, that wild flowers given her by small children were kept until they fell apart.

"As I look back, I realize that I didn't go to visit my own mother often enough when she was living," Betty admits. "I know now that my not coming made it harder for my sister-in-law who was caring for her. I wonder how many people think about this."

That is something for all of us to remember, I thought, whether we are able to have our elders with us in our home, or if they are living elsewhere.

We discussed the fact that the stories most sharply remembered by Grandmother were of long ago, of her early marriage, how she helped to deliver babies, tragedies, and triumphs she had lived through.

"These old stories are what keep them alive," Betty analyzed. "When they're not able to do those things any longer, they can remember. Most of the stories Grandmother tells are from the years when she was active and involved, when she was helping other people. We're all that way about the important times in our lives, when we were making a contribution. Her stories of frontier times interest my young neighbors, and one neighbor was quite excited to learn that an old house Grandmother had lived in was being restored."

Speaking of the neighbors, Betty told me all the children of the neighborhood enjoyed being around a grandparent, just as her own children did. Grandmother would often sit on the porch and watch a ball game, and the kids appreciated their audience.

"They get along so well. They don't fight," Grandmother would remark, to which the family would laugh and say, "Grandmother, you're lucky you're deaf. They're like a bunch of blackbirds. They fight and don't have an umpire."

"But just having Grandmother sitting there gives them a good feeling," I reflected. "I think that is tremendous. You really have a rare situation."

"Well, you see, she's a rare person," Betty pointed out. "But I'm only giving you the good side of things. Of course, you know life isn't always like that. Everyone has his ups and downs and blue days, when nothing seems right. I don't share with Grandmother the little arguments that come up in the family, or anything she might worry about, because those things always blow over. And it's a funny thing, Grandmother can't see anything but good in her grandchildren. I wish everybody could be that way about other people!"

Betty described where Grandmother's grandchildren were now scattered all over the world. She was delighted when they could go away to college, and right now she was happy about Jimmy's musical tour. "She has a real sense of humor," Betty said, "and that's why the grandchildren are so fond of her."

As for the youth culture, Betty's large house was an advantage. Grandmother was far enough away from the record player, that she was not bothered by the music. And she could always take off her hearing aid! Even the occasional grandchild who sported a moustache or let his hair grow longer did not make her uptight. Unaware of the protest movement and its implications, changing hairstyles simply reminded her of another generation, when men, including her own husband, wore beards and moustaches and looked "nice."

"These older persons worked hard in their time," Betty continued. "The most they could get was a living, and they didn't worry about accumulating things. They took care of what they had, but they were more interested in people, and I think that and her deep faith in God accounts for the way Grandmother is now."

"I see your life as rich, Betty, in fact, unique. Did you have to struggle at all with the idea of taking in the older generation?"

"There was never any question that we wanted to do it," she said thoughtfully. "I don't think it's the responsibility of the state or the country to take care of our parents, if we are able to do it. Even if we don't have too much, we can give them what we have. But I know that what has worked out happily for us might not work for everyone in every circumstance. I give a lot of credit to Ralph, who was easily satisfied with decisions made by the grandparents or by me. Then, too, our house was large enough for privacy and we had endless chores to keep everyone busy."

I asked Betty what principle she felt most helpful in getting along together and she laughingly replied, "Do unto others as you would like them to do unto you."

As we talked, one by one other members of the family began to appear in the doorway, hearing the train of thought and joining in.

Barbara said, "At school I see kids who have never

been close to their grandparents, and they feel that when people are old they should be put in institutions. But I can see that the whole of an old person's life is remembering and being with people who are important to him. After all, if it weren't for Grandmother, none of us would be here! Since I have always been around older people, I feel more compassion for them, even the ones who come into the bank."

"Do you remember anything about the death of your grandfather?" I wondered, knowing that he had died at home.

"It seemed a natural thing, like sleep, for he had been in a coma before his death. It didn't give me any fears."

Ralph also entered and joined the reminiscing about his parents. He had a favorite story to tell about Granddaddy.

"One day he was working on the roof," he said, "when one of his granddaughters screamed as though she was really hurt. He climbed down the ladder and when he saw that her scream was without good reason, he told her, 'I bet the next time you holler, you'd better be hurt!' "

We discussed the fact that everyone in this house was a part of the mainstream of life, and Betty said, "It hasn't always been easy, but I know it hasn't hurt our children."

Barbara teased, "Yes, if it weren't for that, we might put you away somewhere when you're old."

Betty rejoined, "That's what I'm thinking about, Barbara."

Linda, appearing during the laughter that followed, had only one thing on her mind.

"I'm hungry, Mom."

So we headed again for the kitchen. But I wanted a last word with Grandmother, and before I left I visited her in her room.

She showed me the windowsill, where she fed the birds in the winter and kept a count of the squirrels-in-residence. She showed me all her family pictures, including the portrait of her little daughter, whose death had been so difficult for her.

"At first, I blamed myself," she told me, "but one day I opened my heart to God and He spoke to me. I saw that He was King."

And then she told me a story that I knew had to be more than eighty years old. "I want to tell you how I first learned about God," she said. "I used to crawl into the cradle with my baby brother and rock him to sleep. Then I would fall asleep myself. One day, when I awoke, my mother came over to the cradle and said, as she patted me, 'God bless my children.'"

A century of love, I thought, love passed from generation to generation, kaleidoscoped before my very eyes.

"You are a beautiful person, Grandmother," I said, as we went out to join the children and the children's children waiting in the next room.

Barbara Sowell: It's such a blessing to have perfect babies, and then to find out they are gifted as well.

The Rhythm of Her Days

Several years before I rang Barbara Sowell's doorbell, I heard her sing. It was a capacity crowd at a
conference on missions, and in her rich, resonant
contralto, accompanied by a youth group playing two
guitars and a bass fiddle, she sang a song of her own
making. Written to the tune of a current television
theme song, one verse went:

There's a mansion in the sky
In the sweet by-and-by
For the Christian (dependable Christian).
In the Bible it is told
Heaven's streets are made of gold
For the Christian (peaceable Christian).
It's a land so bright and fair,
If you want to meet me there,
Be a Christian (merciful Christian).

There followed other songs which Barbara had written to familiar tunes, one of which was hard to for-

get. After telling the story of the demons which Jesus transferred from the wild man among the tombs to the herd of hogs, we heard the former hog owners say:

I want my hogs, Lord, I don't like lamb.
I like my bacon, and I love my ham.
I want my hogs, Lord! You killed them dead.
I spent my money — nearly all I had.

Later when Leamon, her pastor husband, led in a devotional, he told the audience, "I just can't understand it. My wife and I live under the same roof, we eat the same food, and we read the same Bible, but no songs come to me as they do to her."

When I finally rang Barbara's doorbell, I was greeted at the door of their brown brick apartment house in Maywood, a west suburb of Chicago, by two Sowells, Barbara and her preschooler Becky. Becky added her sparkle to the entire visit, and was not really in the way. It was obvious that she and her mother operated on the same wavelength. She played the piano for me (reading the music), showed me that she could read and could write a little, and sometimes told her mother's favorite stories before she could tell them herself. When she did not understand something she overheard, she would ask a sensible question. However, her four-year-old ears did not catch the meaning of everything she heard. When Barbara explained that her husband was attending a meeting on *crisis*, Becky quickly chirped, "That reminds me of '*Christ is* the answer.'"

Barbara told me that all of her children were able to read before they entered school, and one child was reading on a third-grade level before he went to first grade. How had she accomplished this?

She was clearly ahead of *Sesame Street* with her young children. "I use rhyme, rhythm, and tune when I teach them," she explained. Becky, for instance, knew her telephone number in the form of a cheer, her address, 811 South Fifteenth Avenue, in a little ditty which Barbara invented. All her children learned early to spell their own names. Using a little book with the alphabet illustrated with birds and animals, they had learned their letters by associating pictures and a special song written by their mother. After that Barbara would make out a word list for each letter, composing whole sentences in which each word began with a given letter.

"It was a game — they didn't even know they were learning," she said. "I taught them at the laundromat or at home while I was doing other things. Becky, recite the books of the Bible for Mrs. Brenneman."

I listened amazed while the little miss chanted the library of biblical books clearly and without faltering.

"I was teaching the youth class at the Bethel Church to memorize the books of the Bible with rhythm, and Becky learned by listening," Barbara said.

While we sat chatting in the living room of their second-floor apartment, Barbara told me about their other children. Leamon Junior, 16 and a high school senior, was attending a church school in Iowa. Zenobia, who was named after a black Egyptian queen said to be more beautiful than Cleopatra, was fourteen and also in high school. Debbie, 10, was in fifth grade and would soon be home for lunch, and Becky, of course, was four. The new baby was expected in October, just a month away.

"Sounds like you have a planned family," I noted.

"Not exactly," she smiled. "The Lord planned our family for us. "Already I was observing a pattern in Barbara's speech, a spontaneous recital of the ways of the Lord and her daily conversations with Him. Typical of such statements were: "The Lord worked it out Himself. This is what the Lord did. It took the Lord to do it. I said this to the Lord. He said that to me."

The words, "Hitherto hath the Lord helped me," seemed neatly to sum up anything she had to say. Once I asked her about answers to prayer, and she threw up her hands and cried, "Answers to prayer? Where would I start?"

I knew that husband Leamon (pronounced Lēman — "the a keeps him from being sour") served as pastor of the Bethel Mennonite Church and was in charge of the Chicago Team Ministry of several churches. But I didn't know where the family had served or where they had lived before moving to their present home. I learned that Leamon was already pastoring a Church of God congregation when Barbara met him, that their first home was a high-rise apartment in the area where the Bethel Church was located, and that they had served that church for eight years after a period as assistant pastor in a downtown congregation.

As Barbara recalled her first years of married life, she told me about the variety of places where they had lived. During the years when the first two children were small, their home had been a basement apartment.

"Those were difficult years. The apartment was so wet that our clothes molded. When Deborah was born, we moved in with my mother for a while."

The high-rise buildings, in the middle of the Grace Abbot project, were something else. One hundred fifty families lived on fifteen floors of each building, and "if you don't think that means problems, you should live there and see," she told me.

Looking around at her cheerful apartment, Barbara again praised God. "Getting this house was a miracle," she said. "The house was up for sale, and a friend of mine lived here. When she said, 'Why don't you buy this?' Leamon said her question was like asking, 'Why don't you buy the moon?' "

Barbara described a series of circumstances — loans, cosigners, prayers, and there was that affirmation again: "The Lord gave us this place." She went on to tell how Christian friends had decorated for them and a number of churches had cooperated in remodeling her kitchen.

We were interrupted when a young mother knocked at the door and peered around it to say, "I was in the neighborhood, and I just had to stop."

"Do you get many callers?" I asked, after she and her child had gone on their way.

"Not as many as we had when we lived in the high-rise apartments," she said, "but the telephone about rings off the hook some days."

"How did you get started writing songs?" I asked, wanting to get back on the subject of her creativity.

She explained that on a trip to Battle Creek, Michigan, she had heard a cigarette ditty on the radio and said to herself, "That is a nice tune. And since every good and perfect gift comes from God, whether people give Him glory for it or not, what would be wrong with using such a tune for His glory?"

The words which came to her at that time were the beginning of a flood. For three weeks she could not stop writing lyrics, and during that time she completed a whole book of songs.

"The inspiration would leave me if I didn't write it down, and I did not want to lose those beautiful thoughts. But sometimes I almost thought I was losing my mind! Then I realized that I was so stubborn, that the Lord had to make quite an impression on me before He could get my attention. Now it has slowed down, but the songs still come."

I inquired how I could purchase one of Barbara's records, "Be a Christian," and learned that one could be obtained in exchange for a contribution to the "Compassion Fund," a sum set aside for the ministry of the church to minorities.

Writing songs climaxed a life of creativity for Barbara, who was born and reared near Wheaton, Illinois, one of seven children of a factory worker.

"I attended an almost all-white school in Glen Ellyn," she said, "and the few black families had a time making their way, because many of the white people there hadn't met up with black people before. You could tell by the children what their parents' attitude was until they got into high school. Then it seemed that the children made up their own minds. We did have some hardships. When we were playing games, if someone had to be left out, it was always us. And I can remember a girl calling out over and over, "Hello, nigger!" Yet I did have my friends.

"When I was about Becky's age, I had a remarkable memory. In school they would give me the long pieces to memorize on programs, and I enjoyed dramatics. Now what has happened to that beautiful memory?" she chuckled.

"How old are you now, Barbara?"

"Thirty-seven, but I still enjoy drama."

She told of an interdenominational group in her neighborhood which occasionally put on plays, and that she had played the part of a grandmother in one entitled "Unequally Yoked Together."

Becky, who had been engaged in a string of playful patter, interrupted to say, "Hi, Mommy."

Barbara responded with a warm, "Hi, Becky," then dipped back into her childhood memories.

"I accepted Christ when I was nine years old, partly out of fear because of a carpenter who wanted to marry my sister and threatened to blow up our house. I decided to turn to God for help."

But after Barbara's decision to follow Christ, she found that her vivid imagination got her into trouble.

"I was an exaggerating liar over the years. I could hardly tell any story straight. And I just had to come face-to-face with the fact that exaggerating is just plain lying. It frightened me to think that liars would not enter the kingdom of heaven. I made New Year's resolutions, but it didn't do any good. And here, I had been in Sunday school all my life and everybody thought I was such a wonderful Christian. They didn't know I was in such torment. Really, I was desperate.

"Then, when I was nineteen, not long before I got married, I began to claim the Word of God. I realized that the Scripture says, 'Sin shall not have dominion over you. You are not under the law, but under grace.' I saw that I had been trying to overcome that sin in my own strength."

There followed a conversation between Barbara and the Lord which went something like this:

Barbara: "Lord, I know the Scripture says, 'Whom the Lord forgives much will love much.' I must not love You very much, or else I could quit telling these lies. Perhaps I've been too good all my life except for that habit. If You don't stop me, I'm going out and do a lot of other things. Then maybe I can come back to You for forgiveness and can overcome them all. If You don't stop me, people will find out and Your name will be shamed."

The Lord: "Well, Barbara, it's not necessary to do that."

(Barbara tried to tell me what happened, but she couldn't really explain it. "I don't know where it went, but anyway, it's gone! The Lord freed me and gave me in place of that habit a great love for the truth. I am so grateful, for no one knows how miserable I was. I could have become a mental case.")

Barbara continued the conversation between herself and the Lord.

The Lord: Now Barbara, whenever you see anyone

in any kind of sin, whether drunkenness or anything they're steeped in, just remember that if it hadn't been for grace, that could have been you."

Barbara: "OK, Lord, it's a deal."

Barbara concluded her story by saying, "Now I have a great compassion for people who have a habit they can't break."

"And now you feel you are using your imagination for a better purpose?" I asked.

"I suppose that is what the Lord is using when I write these songs," she responded. "He had to take it and curb it His way."

"In other words, you have a sanctified imagination."

"I like that way of saying it."

Having worked our way through Barbara's autobiography to her meeting Leamon, I waited while Barbara ran for her wedding albums and showed me her pictures.

"I had attended Wheaton College for two years and had begun nurse's training when I met Leamon," she told me. "Dr. Edmond, who was then president of Wheaton — he has now gone to be with the Lord — married us. We had an integrated wedding party. Dr. Edmond, three ushers, the ring bearer, and the flower girl were white, while my three bridesmaids and matron of honor and the best man were black."

Of course, I wanted to know how she had met Leamon, who had grown up in Tennessee, but I was not prepared for what I heard. It seems that a year before Barbara and Leamon met, she had been told in a dream not to marry another young man, for whom there had already been a wedding date set. The

Lord indicated to her that she would meet someone else a year later, and it was exactly one year, to the day, that she married her husband.

Leamon had meanwhile been praying for guidance in finding a wife. At a youth rally, where he had preached, he sought her out to ask her to pray for him. Barbara laughs as she says, "It turned out that I was the answer to his prayer!"

Later on, in the date room of Mt. Sinai Hospital where Barbara was studying to be a registered nurse, Leamon told of his experiences in World War II when, during his service in the army, he had developed convictions which made it impossible for him to carry a gun. His superiors accepted his scruples with respect and gave him an assignment as a medic.

"When I heard his testimony and learned that after getting out of the army he had kept his promise to God to go to Bible school and study for the ministry, I sensed that he was real. And I thought he must have been pretty precious in the Lord's sight to have been protected from so much danger while he was serving as a medic on the front in Europe. I decided to count him precious in my sight, too."

Because Barbara met Leamon when she had only three months of nurse's training, she decided that God had brought her to Chicago for a purpose other than her intended career. Eleven years later she did complete her training as a licensed practical nurse and worked for a year when her parents and grandparents were sharing her home and were able to look after the children.

"How do you feel about your life as a wife and

mother?" I inquired, having heard that some of our black sisters do not have the same problem with role and identity that some of their white friends struggle with.

In a way, the question seemed superfluous. Barbara had already described in detail her joy with her family, her pleasure in teaching the children and watching them mature.

"It's such a blessing to have perfect babies," she rejoiced aloud, "and then to find out that they are gifted as well."

She described a period in the life of her family when she had assigned a chapter from the Bible each day to her children, asking them to summarize and be quizzed on its contents, then grading them according to age. They had worked from Genesis through Leviticus, and "we never had such meaningful devotions as we did at that time." Although the children earned cameras as an incentive for their progress, a "Tribute to Mother" speech, which Leamon Junior had recently given in a church meeting on Mother's Day, brought tears to Barbara's eyes and assured her that there were greater rewards than the material awards.

I passed on a compliment to Barbara which a mutual friend had given her, after having worked for several years alongside the Sowells. He had told me that he felt Barbara and Leamon were equally effective in the community and church, and that he had not sensed a pattern of dominance in their family life.

Barbara did not argue with that, although she

admitted, "Leamon and I sometimes disagree sharply on some issues."

"But he allows you to disagree?"

She smiled and nodded. "One time, when he could not attend a national church committee meeting at O'Hare Travelodge, he sent me in his place. I enjoyed it, and the men on the committee seemed to appreciate his asking me to do it."

As for her contribution to the church, Barbara has spent many hours teaching church school classes, vacation Bible school, and youth groups. She leads a Bible study class for ladies who live near the church and has joined others from the congregation in knocking on doors and becoming acquainted with families in the high-rise apartment buildings.

Because many of the people in this area move frequently, building a permanent Christian community is an uphill climb. "There's plenty of room for more at our church, I can tell you," Barbara said, in describing their church membership. But she went on to point out other contacts which the Bethel Church has with its neighbors, not the least of which is a day-care center for children of working mothers, located in the church building.

"I have had a dream for fifteen years," Barbara told me, "but you know, I prayed for a piano for seventeen years before the Lord answered my prayer, and so I have hope. Our young people need a place where they can go for recreation. I dream of building a church-sponsored roller skating rink on a big lot near the church. Suppose that different churches would take turns as hosts and there would be trained personal workers on wheels, as well as occasional inspirational speakers. Suppose. . . ."

What about her personal dreams? Barbara likes private duty nursing, and she hopes to do more writing when the children are older and make less demands on her time. But she is in no hurry for all of this. In the meantime she lives by rhyme, rhythm, and tune and there is a rhythmic pattern to her days, new songs on her heart, and a joy in creativity which she takes as a gift from God.

Lydia Shank: I tried to treat the children as their mother would have. To be her successor was an honor.

Not a Stepmother

I began ringing Lydia Shank's doorbell when, as a young bride, I discovered our cousinhood. Actually, this gracious lady was a second cousin to my father. Living in the same Midwestern town, we felt drawn to one another and liked to get together to talk.

It was during the years that I was working on my PHT degree (Put Hubby Through) that Lydia asked me to help her with a typing job as she edited a monthly informational and prayer sheet for the women's organization of her denomination. I gladly helped her each month, as I enjoyed observing the warm relationship which she maintained with members of a family to whom she had in recent years become a second mother. And I liked the good lunch which was always a fringe benefit on the day I helped Lydia.

I remember wondering one day why Lydia had slipped off and changed her clothes when she had been perfectly groomed on my arrival, then suddenly realized that her sister Lillie was in the house. Identical twins, Lydia and Lillie could sometimes fool even their best friends.

Now, almost twenty-five years later, I called on Lydia in her pleasant apartment in a retirement villa, and I had so many things to ask her, I hardly knew where to start. The admiration which I had felt for her as a young wife had proved to be well-founded.

When I first met Lydia, she had been a second mother to the family of Charles Shank for almost ten years. Since none of the family has allowed her to be called a stepmother, the six children, plus a foster daughter living in their home, called her "Mother" with real affection. Now, when I asked for an interview for this book, Charles was no longer living, and all seven of their children were scattered throughout the world, some as full-time missionaries, the others as responsible members of church and community. I had to wait for my interview until Lydia returned from a visit to her daughter Lois (Mrs. Glenn Musselman) and family in Brazil. When I walked into her apartment, there was still an aura of excitement about her.

I had heard her give her testimony at church the Sunday before, and I was impressed when she told me that when asked if she had traveled alone she had replied, "I bought only one ticket, but I did not travel alone." Then she had gone on to describe how each lap of the trip had been accompanied by a sense of Providence, including meeting someone at the end who could speak the native Portuguese and help her through customs with the musical equipment which she was taking to her daughter and family. Even the weather had been favorable, and Lydia mentioned that extremes of hot and cold had seemingly waited until after her departure, both in the States and in the land to the south.

"Now, Lydia," I teased, "do you mean to tell me that God rearranged the weather in a whole hemisphere just for your benefit?"

She had to think a bit before her rebound: "No, He didn't change the weather for me. He just fit my trip into the existing weather conditions."

The thing that always impressed me about Lydia was the way her life fell into meaningful sequences and her skill in making the transition from one chapter to another. A schoolteacher until she was thirty-nine, she had taught on three levels, elementary, secondary, and college. When she married, her role as mother was of primary importance to her, but even during those busy years she managed to carry a small teaching load. Then, when her time was free again for teaching, she had returned to college and had added a certificate in elementary education to her master's degree. During the years that followed she had taught English to two of my children. Then there had been a period of retirement for her and her engineer husband, followed now by an adjustment to widowhood.

During all these years Lydia and her twin had kept in touch, although Lillie was a medical doctor and Lydia a teacher of French and English. Both had attended the University of Virginia, both pursued their careers with an intensity based on their caring about people, and after satisfying years of concentrated service, both married widowers who had been missionaries to India. A difference in their marriage was that Lillie's husband no longer had children at home when he married her, while Lydia's new family consisted of six children between the ages of nine and nineteen.

Lydia and Lillie grew up on a dairy farm near Elida, Ohio, in a family where there were two other sisters and a brother. The family was education-minded, which surprised me even though I knew Lydia graduated from college the year I was born.

"Weren't you an unusual family in your community those days?" I asked, after she described how she and Lillie had cooperated in supporting one another through college, taking turns working for room and board and living in the dormitory, and that she had taught for one year midway through her college experience.

"Yes," she smiled, "people throught we were proud. But actually, my grandfather Shenk had been a schoolteacher, and my mother's mother wrote a book of poetry which was published after her death. Both of my parents believed in education, but my mother talked more about it. She wished so much she could have a good education."

When Lydia's twin entered Women's Medical College in Philadelphia, she had a strong determination to become a missionary doctor, and Lydia took a teaching position at Manasses, Virginia, near Washington, D.C., partly to help her through medical school. By that time their parents had settled in Virginia, which was how it happened that they attended the University of Virginia at Charlottesville.

"I was glad to help Lillie because I knew she wanted to be a missionary," Lydia explained, "but Lillie was deeply disappointed when an examining physician told her that she was not physically strong enough at the time to be a foreign missionary. But later, after she had practiced in a home for delinquent girls for three years, she was asked by a mission board to go to Africa, where she served another five years before meeting her husband, J. N. Kaufman. Six years later they worked together in India, Lillie in charge of medical work and J. N. as bishop and bookkeeper."

"Lydia," I recalled, "I remember your son David telling me how much you twins thought alike. He said it was absolutely uncanny, that one year you gave each other yellow nightgowns for your birthday."

That brought a chuckle, as Lydia told how on another occasion they bought each other red dress material at the same time.

"Even as children it was amazing how we always agreed on things," she said, "and we liked to work together on cleaning or other chores. Our school-teachers used to try to find out which one was the sharper, which was doing the better work, but we wouldn't tell. Of course, it depended somewhat on the subject."

"Did you ever take advantage of teachers' inability to tell you apart?" I wondered.

"A little. One of the grade school teachers put buttons on us, one red and one black, and when he

165

wasn't looking we traded."

Of course, I wanted to know if the twins had ever switched dates, but Lydia assured me that they hadn't, although they discovered years after a fellow who had dated her thought he had dated Lillie.

"It is strange that when we lived in the same community we seemed to look more alike," Lydia reflected. "We had the same gestures and the same laugh. I tended to carry my head higher, while Lillie walked more humbly. It was as though she were always ready to help someone."

Lydia had taught in both elementary and high schools when the president of a small, church-related college in Goshen, Indiana, invited her to join his faculty as a French instructor. During the summers of her eight college-teaching years, she would teach summer school or visit her parents and help them with gardening, painting, and papering. One summer she sailed for England to visit Lillie before she left for Africa. That year she traveled around in Europe with a friend, and the next summer she returned to Europe as a traveling companion to one of her students, again visiting a number of countries and practicing her French.

When Lydia married Charles *Shank*, she changed her name by only one letter, as her maiden name was *Shenk*. But her life-style was changed much more drastically than her name. Charles had been a widower for nine and a half years; a widowed sister cared for his children. Earlier, when his wife, Crissie, was still living, he had served the cause of missions by setting up an industrial plant in India, teaching

166

the people to make useful items. Then when Ruth, their oldest child, became seriously ill, the family had to return to their home community of Orrville, Ohio. Soon Charles joined the Hoover Sweeper Company in North Canton, Ohio, as an inventor and research engineer. Lydia has a sweeper today with the nozzle which Charles invented while he was with the company.

"I did a smart thing when I married Charles Shank," Lydia beamed. "I inherited this good family. There are many people who are much more lonely than I because they have no children."

I told Lydia that I had once heard that when she married Charles, people couldn't tell for sure with whom she was in love most, Charles or his children.

Lydia responded by telling me that both she and Charles were convinced that they had been kept for one another, and that she felt that all her life's experiences had culminated in their marriage.

"Charles had prayed for a companion and mother for his children for a number of years, and sometimes he couldn't understand why God didn't answer his prayers. But after he had me, he was thankful that nothing else had worked out."

"Did the children, as old as they were, feel any resentment at your coming?"

Lydia explained that Charles had prepared the way for her and that both he and the children immediately called her "Mother." Of course, everyone had to adjust to the new title and Lydia to calling Charles "Papa." Later, David expressed his feelings in a letter.

"Sometimes it's easier for people to give words of

appreciation in letter form than to go right up to you and say it. When I got my first letter from David, I had to cry. He told me how much it meant to him to have a mother; when I came into the family, he could go to school and talk about *his* mother. He loved Aunt Sally, but the other children always talked about their mothers. I didn't know that it meant that much to him."

Lydia said that she often gets words of appreciation from her children, and when she was visiting in Brazil, Lois remarked about the change in the home after Lydia arrived. "It was the difference between night and day when you came," she said.

"Aunt Sally had been hesitant to go ahead and do things to beautify the home," Lydia explained. "I bought curtains and draperies. I knew it meant a lot to the family because we did so much entertaining."

Lydia admitted that her life took on a radical change. The children, however, had been assigned chores before she came, and they continued with their share of responsibilities. But instead of going to class, she washed on Monday, ironed on Tuesday, mended on Wednesday, often attended women's meetings on Thursday, and Friday found her beginning preparations for the weekend's entertaining.

I was waiting in vain for some complaint. "Did you miss the mental stimulation of your former career?"

"No, there was plenty to think about with the children. They had their schoolwork, and they were so appreciative of everything I did. Then, after our family moved to Goshen, Indiana, the college asked me to do a bit of teaching, and during the war years I taught some at the high school. I didn't really want to do this, but they kept coming after me. And I did enjoy teaching."

Thus it was that after the first two years of her marriage, Lydia returned to the classroom part time. "We had good family cooperation, and the children were pleased and proud that I was teaching," she said.

Lydia is easily moved to tears or laughter, and both are close to the surface when she talks about her children.

"One thing we don't know," she said with tears in her eyes, "and that is how much those who have gone on ahead observe of our lives. I never told the children this, but I often thought of Crissie watching me take care of her precious children. I sometimes got impatient, but I tried to treat the children as their mother would have treated them. I think if all second mothers would take that attitude, there would be no cruel stepmother stories."

"One thing I always remembered about your life with the Shank family, Lydia," I mentioned, "was how you honored their first mother. There was no spirit of competition."

"I think that was one thing that helped me to be successful with the children, I never knew Crissie myself, but everywhere I went I heard others praise her. Instead of feeling jealous, I took it as a challenge to meet some of her high standards. I felt honored to be her successor."

When Lydia joined the family, Lois was nine (she and Glenn have been missionaries in Brazil for sixteen years). Esther was eleven (she is a dietitian in a hospital in Colorado). David was thirteen (for twenty-one years he and his family have been missionaries in Brussels, Belgium). Ernest was fifteen (he is inventive like his father and works with audio-visual aids in the school system in Sarasota, Florida; he is also an active churchman). Mary was eighteen (she and her husband, Ernest Lehman, now live near Lydia, but spent almost ten years in relief work in Jordan and the Congo). Paul was nineteen (he is now a machinist in Wooster, Ohio, where he serves as a deacon in his church).

Since Mary is the only member of Lydia's family living in our area, and she was already eighteen when a new mother was initiated into the family, I called her after my interview with Lydia and asked for some of her early memories.

"As a college teacher suddenly turned mother, she was worried about the cooking," Mary recalled. "The first meal she fixed was expandable — French Hunter Stew. To this day this is a favorite dish in our family, since it was the first one she cooked for us.

"I was ready to go to college when Mother arrived, and I remember being grateful for her help in shopping for clothes. Then she personally drove me out to college."

When I think of the Charles Shank family, I think of missions. There must have been something in their home life which inspired their children to give their lives to Christ and the church. I asked Lydia about this.

Even though Charles and his family had to return from the mission field because of illness in the family (his daughter Ruth died five years after the death of his wife), he never lost his interest in missions, Lydia told me.

"He was well informed, enjoyed reading about missions, and was a generous contributor," she said. "He often amazed me in how ready he was to give. He passed on his love for the mission field to his children."

"How did he do this?" I had to know.

Lydia described the regular morning worship at the breakfast table, when Charles prayed earnestly for missionaries they knew. And there was the constant entertaining, when missionaries came to their community.

"David wrote once in an article that it was only natural for the children to become missionaries because we had so many in our home. I think people who don't entertain missionaries don't know what they're missing."

And then she told a story which the children who were at home at the time would never forget. "Our pastor's wife arranged for a missionary family from India to visit at our home. Since Charles had to work late that evening, we suggested that they come after supper for refreshments and stay overnight. We cleaned the house and were ready to sit down to potato soup, tomatoes, and grapes when someone noticed a car drive into the neighbor's driveway, and I just knew they were looking for our place and had come for supper.

"I told the children, 'Now, I'm going upstairs to change my dress. You be friendly to them if they come before I get down.' But I made it down before they came in. We all sat and visited a little, then I suggested they might want to walk around outside and look at the flowers while we put the food on the table. They were delighted, because they had been sitting around visiting all day.

"Since I had no meat cooked, I decided to open some salmon, slice tomatoes and cheese, and serve grapes and cake. One of the children told a neighbor about our unexpected guests, and she brought a pie and some cookies to the back door.

"At dinner, I said, 'I thought maybe you've been served so many roasts, that you'd enjoy salmon for a change.' They replied that they appreciated salmon, because they couldn't buy it in India. They never found out that we weren't expecting them for dinner, but Esther, Lois, and David could hardly hold back their amusement at the way we managed."

"Lydia," I injected, "we haven't mentioned Mary Kay. When I used to come and visit you, I admired the way you had taken her in as another member of your family. In fact, I know that you influenced me to add a very welcome teenager to our household a few years later."

"Yes," she recalled, "one morning after the children had left for school a social welfare worker knocked at my door and told me that our family had been recommended for a young girl who needed a home right away. Would we take her in for the weekend, at least? Charles, the children, and I were all in favor of taking her and soon, of keeping her. She had never learned to sing or play the piano, but enjoyed music so much that we gave her piano and voice lessons. We sent her to college in Kansas, where she met her husband, and also to nurse's training in Colorado. Mary Kay and her husband live in Kalamazoo, Michigan, and they have a family of four lovely daughters. Her life has brought joy to our family and our relationship has been an enriching experience."

I looked around Lydia's apartment at the many artifacts which stood for her memories and her present contacts with a family who love her. On the walls were pictures from Belgium and the Mount of Olives. There were bookends and a model church from Brazil. There was a picture of Ernest and Mary Lehman taken on their twenty-fifth wedding anniversary. There were cowbells from Europe hanging over a doorway, furniture the children had made, place mats designed and put together with the help of grandchildren, Belgian horses, Jericho camels.

In the adjoining room was a "golden" chair, presented to Charles at a surprise family gathering on his eightieth birthday. I was reminded of his keen sense of humor when Lydia told me of the poem he recited for the occasion and how his children enjoyed it. "He had learned the verse at the age of three. He had a keen memory," she laughed, as she read:

> *You'd never expect*
> *One of my age*
> *To speak in public*
> *On the stage.*
> *But if I chance*

> *To fall below*
> *Demosthenes or Cicero,*
> *Don't view me with a critic's eye,*
> *But pass my imperfections by.*

Charles had died three years before my visit, at the age of eighty-two. He had spent eight years in retirement, during which time he had kept himself busy with work he enjoyed — his shop, gardening, and lawn. "It was a blessing for Charles when he passed on, because he was so uncomfortable. But separation is always hard," Lydia said.

And there was another separation two years after Charles' death. Lillie, who had practiced medicine in Illinois for eighteen years after her last term as a missionary doctor, had moved with her husband to Goshen and bought a house next to that of her sister, to enjoy the twin relationship in their retirement years. Her husband had died two years before Charles' death. After Lydia became a widow, the twins lived in adjoining apartments at the retirement villa. Lydia and Lillie shared many good memories, until Lillie died.

When I visited Lydia, she was seventy-two and was once more alone, except for her frequent contacts with her children and grandchildren. Her trip to Brazil had been partly occasioned by a prolonged and serious illness of a granddaughter. Although she had now recovered, Lydia felt her visit might be an encouragement to the family. The electronic organ equipment which she took with her was for use in a citywide evangelistic crusade for which her daughter Lois had been asked to play.

"There was my little Lois, playing the organ for thousands of people," Lydia said. "I thought, 'If only her brothers and sisters could see her now!' "

Lydia could not speak Portuguese, but felt a smile went a long way. She accompanied Glenn and Lois in visits to the homes of their friends, observed the customs of the people, and noted how the Musselmans were accepted by the people with whom they lived and worked. And she got reacquainted with her "Brazilian" grandchildren. On her return trip she stopped off in Florida and Ohio to visit her sons, Ernest and Paul, and their families.

An advantage of living close to Goshen College has been the presence of grandchildren who come for their college days. At this writing a granddaughter from Florida and two grandsons from Belgium frequent Lydia's apartment, bringing their friends and enjoying her good cooking. Lydia keeps an accurate record of the birthdays of all nineteen of her grandchildren, remembering them with cards and gifts.

Having taken a number of writing courses throughout her life, Lydia renewed her interest in writing in recent years, joined a writers' fellowship group, and began writing articles for the local paper. Other involvements which interest her, besides traveling and entertaining, are a book review club, a prayer fellowship, and church-related activities.

Yes, Lydia, I thought as I left her apartment, you did a smart thing when you married Charles Shank. Your life is rich. And he was not so stupid when he married you, providing his family with a true mother.

Doris Kramer: At Raymond's death, a special strength came on me. I think God's grace is equal to whatever need one has.

She Leans on God

The occasion was a graduation party and there were approximately fifty guests. But the guest of honor was not a teenager. Doris Kramer graduated from a community college at the age of 47, nine years after her husband had died in the prime of his career as a Christian minister, leaving her with a family of seven children.

The years since Raymond's death had not been easy, and it had taken real courage to go back to school when Doris felt her four sons and three daughters were old enough to help her manage an academic schedule.

Doris showed me her scrapbook the day I rang her doorbell, a volume stuffed with clippings of highlights of her life in the little agricultural village of St. Jacobs, eight miles north of Kitchener, Ontario.

"I call this my 'ego book,' " she smiled, while she tidied up the kitchen and put away the dishes. "I continually struggle with feeling terribly inadequate, as though I appear to other people like a blob or something. I keep this book, to boost my spirits."

As I read the program for her graduation party, which had taken place three months before my visit, Doris told me how it came about, how meaningful it was to her whole family. Her good friend Pat had arranged it. Pat's husband had been master of ceremonies, deacon Walter had prayed the dedicatory prayer, and her parents, present from Ohio, had taken a significant part. After her father had given a speech on "Father of the Graduate," her mother had placed the red graduation band across her shoulder. When Grandma and Grandpa Miller sang a duet, one of her sons later said that he had to blink back the tears.

There had been a "Mother Song" by Doris' three daughters, Phyllis, Stephanie, and Mary Ette, a piano solo by one of the children, a vocal solo by her oldest son, Jonathan, and a hymn, "Joyful, Joyful," by all the children, who enjoy singing together. There had been a poem by her friend Pat and an opportunity for words of appreciation. But one of the most memorable speeches was delivered by 18-year-old Marcus, on "Son of the Graduate" or "What It's Like to Have Your Mother Going to School."

"Marcus said that he had mixed feelings about his mother going back to school," Doris recalled, "for it would mean that I had to be gone a lot. But he felt really good now that his mother had a job.

" 'I always had some kind of strings attached to me,' he said. 'First, I was a preacher's kid, then my father died and I was from a one-parent family, and that wasn't right. And then, to top it off, we were on welfare.' "

Doris chuckled as she remembered how he had thrown out his chest in closing the talk. "It feels pretty good to have Mother have a real, honest job to support us, like other families. We can even have ice cream more often now."

Of course, everyone laughed, and the program ended with opening of gifts and Doris' thank-you speech.

"I enjoy gifts," Doris said, in thinking over the big day. "I will never have a 25th or 50th wedding anniversary. But the gift of love and friendship is so beautiful, and I really felt warm inside."

As I examined Doris' "ego book," I found newspaper clippings describing her husband's ministry at Meadville, Pennsylvania, where he served as pastor for twelve years before they came to Ontario, his installation at the 400-member congregation at St. Jacobs, and his sudden passing with cancer in 1962, four years after they moved to Canada. The scrapbook also contained reports on talks which Doris had given in churches, an appointment which she had accepted to a national women's missionary organization, activities of the children, a description of her parents' 50th wedding anniversary, letters to editors and other vignettes she had written, and several articles written about Doris and her family.

In addition, there were letters of appreciation from churches where she had spoken and from friends who took time out to affirm her at crucial moments, and there were cards and notes from her children. I was particularly fascinated by a Father's Day card she had received from Stephanie with the inscription, "I appreciate the leadership you give as 'head of our household.' "

Doris' "ego book" spoke volumes about her concern for others. One clipping, describing her adjustments as a widow, noted, "She believes in sharing her faith as she shares herself."

Since I was in Canada with my family attending a churchwide assembly, I spent a day and two nights at Doris' house, squeezing in an interview between her goings and comings. It wasn't easy. The Social Services diploma, which she had received at the Conestoga College of Applied Arts and Technology, had qualified her for social work, and she was carrying a case load of thirty-four foster children, working on adoption procedures for four. Besides that, she was an elected delegate to the General Assembly we were attending, and had to work in details of living between appointments.

In spite of all this, Doris did not seem to lose her composure. She would come in the door, laughing and talking with her son and two daughters who were still living at home. And one morning she left me a note in the kitchen with instructions as to when to put the roast and baking potatoes in the oven, and to check with my family as to whether they could join us all for dinner that night. They did, and you would have thought our younger teenagers had known one another for years.

Actually, Doris' family unit had shrunk, with two boys away from home for the entire year and a son and daughter working and living elsewhere for the summer. Doris knew that she could expect this kind of mobility, with her children now ranging in years from thirteen to twenty-three.

"And how old were the children when Raymond died?" I asked, when Doris found time to sit and talk.

She told me that her youngest was four and her oldest fourteen when their father called them, one by one, into the hospital room, laid his hand on each as he prayed a parting blessing and gave them an opportunity to express their feelings. Several had asked forgiveness for little disobediences. It had been an unforgettable experience.

"I felt the children made a remarkable adjustment," Doris said, "partly because most of our grief was worked through in the months Raymond was ill." She remembered that one son had more trouble than the others, finding it difficult to sleep at night. And her youngest daughter had felt cheated in school competitions, when classes got credit for bringing the most parents to home and school meetings. But all of them felt free to speak of their father, of what he did or thought, and to talk to God about him.

The passing of husband and father drew the Kramers together as a family unit. Doris noticed that her older children were showing kindness and consideration to the younger ones, and although she did not expect it of him, her oldest son Jonathan automatically assumed the role of a "father figure" to the little ones. Looking back, Doris wonders whether so much responsibility was not pretty heavy for a boy in his early teens.

"Father's Day was always hard," Doris pointed out, "because Raymond died on Father's Day, 1962. Society is geared to two-parent families."

Doris realizes that she had some advantages over many widows because of the love which Raymond's congregation demonstrated to the family both before and after his death. When the seriousness of his illness became apparent, organized love released her to be with him at the hospital. At home the children were cared for, hot meals arrived on time, the house received both a weekly and a seasonal cleaning, and soiled laundry disappeared and came back washed, ironed, and mended. At the hospital volunteer nurses helped prepare Raymond for the night.

When her husband was gone, Doris kept telling herself that the help she had been receiving could not go on indefinitely. But the St. Jacobs Church did not forget her. Over the years her friends kept her furnished with garden produce, and one year she was able to can and freeze 700 quarts of fruits and vegetables. Besides this, trusted men in the church cosigned her checks, helped her with insurance, and guided her in making decisions as to the purchase of a car and its maintenance and other practical matters.

Doris laughed when I asked her how she manages her budget problems. "I don't keep books, I just can't. But I file my bills systematically, and put away money to pay my taxes. Somehow I have managed not to go into debt."

The Kramers had always lived in parsonages. Fortunately, however, Raymond had provided Doris with an insurance policy which she was advised to use in building a house. Although a debt-free home was a tremendous asset, Doris was still obliged to accept welfare for the family's daily living expenses.

"It was provincial welfare and was dignified by being called 'Family Benefits.' But I found it a humiliating experience and very hard to take. It affects your feeling of worth, because people on welfare are talked about as being parasites, no-good people — over-generalizations, of course. And the fact that we had a big family fit into the image."

"Did the children suffer economically?" I wanted to know.

"I didn't feel that the children were terribly deprived. They have all taken piano lessons and two have finished grade eight in piano. They play other instruments and sing. Jon and Dan play guitars semiprofessionally. I have told the children they are rich, but they always felt poor because they wore secondhand clothes. Although they probably have had more and better clothes than we could have afforded, they have had very few new ones, even today."

She paused to reflect. "I know how they feel, because even though Jesus said if we have food and clothes we should be content, I have sometimes had the desire to go in and choose something suitable to my personality."

Doris has had little ways of augmenting her income. She earned community concert tickets for herself and some of her children by typing up membership cards and selling other memberships. And there are the public speaking appointments which come to her regularly from both her own denomination and the United Church of Canada.

"God has given me the gift of communicating with people, and often someone will come to me after a service and say, 'I didn't know you'd have a struggle in that area.' I'm very down-to-earth and not terribly profound or creative, but I like to share."

Early in my visit I mouthed the platitude, "Now don't go to any fuss while I'm here."

Her answer was quick and definite.

"Don't worry. I have too much company for that." She told me that a few days before she had come in from work and found eight people eating dinner at her table. Two of her sons, living away from home, had brought guests and were serving the meal.

This reminded me of something I had read in her "ego book," part of a printed talk she had given on hospitality. On one occasion, after a four-hour notice from a son working in a coffeehouse that he was bringing fifteen guests, she had ended up with twenty-five. One of the children had exclaimed, "My mother would have walked out!"

Doris still laughs at her shift in values after she built her house. Having never had a new home before, she determined that she would require her children to enter by the basement and remove their shoes before coming upstairs to the main floor. This procedure did not last long. Doris decided that her home should be neither a showplace nor a museum place. It was to be lived in and shared.

And it has been, bulging at its seams with young people, her own friends, and foreign students.

Five years before, she and her friend Pat had become involved in a hosting program for international students attending the University of Waterloo and Waterloo Lutheran College. That began a series of friendships which enriched her family life, broke down or prevented barriers of prejudice, and helped the entire family to understand other cultures.

Over the years there were a Jamaican student who came every Sunday for dinner, a young Pakistani fellow who called her his Canadian mother and asked her to mail out wedding invitations for him, students who brought their own records and performed their native dances in her living room, friends from Uganda, Ghana, Rhodesia, the West Indies, a princess from Swaziland. Since Pat lived on a farm, they had collaborated on sleigh rides and maple sugar productions.

"It doesn't seem as though you have had much time to be lonely," I observed.

"I do fear loneliness in my old age," Doris admitted. "Now that the children are beginning to leave home, I realize that when they are all gone, much of the activity around the house will go with them. When I was a child I experienced real loneliness, and little feelings of loneliness creep back now and then. Probably the times I feel it the most are occasions such as New Year's Eve, when parties are geared to couples, or in a crowd where there are a lot of couples present."

Doris recalled her wish of a few years before to have her own party on New Year's Eve, "but I guess I wanted to feel a little sorry for myself that time." As for parties planned for widows and singles, she finds them a bit inadequate because "I have moved so much with women that I like to be with men and hear their point of view."

When it comes to supportive friendships, Doris considers herself fortunate. The church of which Raymond had been pastor formed a caring community around her family. She joined an ecumenical Bible study group and developed close attachments there. And there are Pat and John, who have shared special occasions with her family: vacations, Christmas, or the day she and her children became Canadian citizens.

"Pat and John never made me feel like a fifth wheel," Doris told me. "We've been very close, and one thing I appreciate is that my children like them so well."

"How about your relationship with others who were friends of yours and Raymond's? Did you feel isolated after your status was changed to that of widow?"

"From the very beginning I determined that I was not going to pity myself," she responded, "because if you're miserable yourself, you're going to go around making everybody else miserable and they don't even want to be with you. I think I have been given special grace from God for this."

She went on. "I had always been a very emotional person, and I was very dependent on Raymond. But at Raymond's death a special strength came to me, so that my sister remarked, 'Doris, this just isn't like you.' I can only say that I think God's grace is equal to whatever need one has. While I formerly leaned on Raymond, now I was forced to lean on God.

"Sometimes I have been tempted to ask, 'Why should this happen to me?' But I found that didn't get me anywhere. So instead, I say, 'What are You trying to say to me, Lord? What do You want me to learn?' "

"And what does He want you to learn?" I asked.

"Well, I became more sensitive to other people's feelings, and I learned I can identify with people who are alone, which I think is important. I learned what friends can do. I honestly have to say that through difficulty I grew and matured, and became a person in my own right."

This reminded me of a comment which I noticed in Doris' scrapbook, penned on her social services diploma: "Doris' teachers have been unanimous in recognizing her sensitivity, ability to empathize, her warmth, relational ability, and compassion for people. She has performed at above-average level."

Doris had described for me some of her school experiences: her initial feeling of nervousness and fear of being a misfit, the release which she had experienced in certain classroom role-playing situations, where her emotional side had a chance to argue with the intellectual side of her being. In dialogue with others and in sharing her innermost feelings, she had grown in the ability to accept herself.

Doris knew that she had matured in some ways as a result of Raymond's death, because she had to develop her own resources. "In a way Raymond had been liberating me as a person before he died," she evaluated. "He had been receiving valuable insights in a school of pastoral care so that I believe he would have continued to encourage me to be myself. I have found quite a bit of fulfillment as a person, even as a person alone. I feel sometimes that if I could talk to Raymond, he would be pleased with me. Or maybe he is — maybe he knows. Yet I feel I still have a lot of room for growth. I want to keep on growing and changing."

Doris thought over some of the special problems which a widow faces, the cessation of a satisfying sexual and emotional relationship with her husband, not much talked about, but very real.

"I suppose the thing I miss the very most is being special to someone," she said. "Raymond pampered me, made much of important occasions, emphasized the surprise element of special days. I know my children love me, but it's not special in the same way as in the marriage relationship."

And there is, of course, the heavy responsibility of being both a mother and a father to one's growing children. Doris told me that, in spite of difficulties, she had been able to maintain a good relationship with each of her children. I had seen a daughter come and put her arm around her mother as we talked. Doris showed me one of Marcus' love letters which he sometimes left around for her to find and read. Son Paul came in one day, and when I told him that I talked with his mother into the wee hours of the night, he answered that he also comes home and keeps her up until 2:00 a.m.

I had asked Doris how she reasons with her children when they accept values and philosophies which are different from her own. With characteristic honesty she said, "I simply tell them, 'This is what has worked for me.' In some cases I knew that I did not use a helpful approach, and I admitted it to them.

"But I am able to sleep at night, even when I am troubled about the children. And I think that is a gift from God."

Doris then shared with me a little ritual which takes place before she gets up every morning. "First I repeat to myself the verse, 'This is the day which the Lord has made. We will rejoice and be glad in it.' And then, while I am still on my back, I commit each of my children to God, beginning with the oldest. If there is a special need, I pray about that.

"Sometimes I have felt selfish, because I spend so much of my prayer time on my children. But I am responsible for them. The thing I have felt so keenly is that I can't be everywhere my children are. I can't do everything for them (and I wouldn't want to). But I believe strongly that the Spirit of God can break through their awareness and remind them of things that they have learned earlier in their lives. It's that kind of faith that helps me to go on living my own life."

When I thought of Doris, leaning on God, I had to smile at the combination of wit and wisdom which often breaks through in conversations with her. She told me of a young fellow-student who accosted her out of class and said, "Oh, Christianity is just a crutch!"

To this our friend replied, "Well, if it is, it's a good one."

Kathryn Swartzendruber: Fulfillment comes as one builds relationships, whether as a farmer's wife or in a regular job.

I Don't Even "Work"

Who can find a satisfied, fulfilled homemaker? Her price these days certainly is far above rubies. That is why I want to introduce to you my friend, Kathryn (Mrs. John D.) Swartzendruber, of rural Goshen, Indiana. Kathryn was asked last summer to speak on "The Rightness of Work as a Means of Fulfillment" at a special Labor Day service at the College Mennonite Church in Goshen.

Although Kathryn is a farmer's wife and a mother of four children, ranging in age from ten to eighteen, those of us who know her think of her in other roles as well. Indeed, we cannot remember when Kathryn was not pouring her energies into summer Bible school, Sunday school (anything from two-year-olds to teenagers), WMSC leadership, MSO Auxiliary, PTO, and Fun Night at the County Home. Not all at one time, of course! And she was voted in as one of the first women on the church's Board of Elders.

At home, however, Kathryn is a full-fledged farmer's wife, one who knows the entire operation of their 120-plus-acre dairy farm. When I rang the doorbell of her spacious farm home, she was being realistic, and not egotistical, when she said, "I'm pretty important. I try to coordinate many activities. I'm official receptionist, telephone-answerer, message-taker and -giver, pump-watcher, and chauffeur." She went on to say that she enjoys haymaking, catching chickens, chasing calves, starting trucks, running tractors, buying parts, painting corncribs, moving irrigation pipes, paying bills, keeping books, and the usual gardening and canning operations of the average rural housewife.

And there is another service which Kathryn performs right in her own home, visiting with and listening to patients of the Oaklawn Psychiatric Center who live with the Swartzendrubers for short periods of time. In all, they have extended hospitality to thirteen patients.

Of John, who also takes an active part in church and community, including serving as volunteer fireman, Kathryn says, "John is easy to live with — maybe he takes out his frustrations on the cows." Thinking about Kathryn, John says, "A farmer with a working wife would be a lonely person." And Kathryn points out that she and John can do many things together during the day, which adds to her contentment.

Of the children Kathryn says, "We try to do a lot of things together as a family. We really enjoy one another." This would include a five-mile hike along an old railroad track, the many swimming parties with other families in the Swartzendruber pond, working together on family projects. All the children play stringed instruments, and when this was written one was in elementary school, one in junior high, one in high school, and one in college.

And now, lest it should happen, as it sometimes does, that the introduction to a speech gets longer than the talk itself, let us listen to Kathryn's reflections on her work as a homemaker.

o   o   o

When I was asked to give this talk, my reaction was, "Why not someone else? I don't even 'work.' " It seems the word *work* has nearly as many meanings as the word *love*. I went to the Bible to see what it had to say, and in looking under "work" in the concordance, I found only the "works of God." So I had to go to the word "labor," which is probably fitting for this Labor Day weekend.

I pondered the theme, "The Rightness of Work as a Means of Fulfillment," as I scrubbed floors, washed dishes, cooked, and mended. And I thought some more, as I painted, raked hay, and fed chickens. With each task came the question, "Am I feeling fulfilled? Does this give me satisfaction?"

It reminded me of a play we had once seen, in which a wife accused her husband of taking his "contentment temperature" so often that he wasn't at ease to enjoy life. Scrubbing floors gives me no great surge of joy, neither does cooking or feeding chickens. Raking hay isn't bad, but I'd not care to do it every day. Do I find fulfillment in my work?

Maybe this talk came at the wrong time, at the end

of a busy summer with no vacation — when I'd had my *fill* of work, rather than feeling *fulfilled!* These and other negative thoughts went through my mind as I faced this subject.

Now, if first of all I could ask all of my family to stand and walk out of the sanctuary, then after they'd left ask anyone else who knows me to leave, I could gather the strangers around me and tell them great tales of my accomplishments and wisdom and give an impressive talk. It would sound good, but of what value would it be? If we are to find fulfillment, we must do a worthy task — something that can be done *honestly* before God and our fellowmen.

I confided in Friend Neighbor about being asked to talk on this subject, and again I asked, "Why me? Wouldn't someone with a 'status' occupation speak more fittingly of the fulfillment he finds in his job?" It seemed it would be more appropriate for a professor, social worker, nurse, or doctor to speak of the satisfaction he or she finds in work.

Well, she chuckled a little, then said, "Someone must know you work like a horse."

Besides not really working that hard, the more I thought about it, the less I liked the comparison. Of course, a horse is strong and works hard, but it can only do what someone else causes it to do, with a blinder at either eye. Satisfaction comes not only in completing a job, but in the planning and in seeing the results. We can be creative! Dinner guests of ours were surprised to see a centerpiece made of onion flowers, globe thistle, and carrot leaves. We look around us and enjoy color and shape. I don't want to plod along with blinders on.

I remember when youngest daughter was small and was watching as I peeled potatoes to make salad. It was near Christmas, and we had the figurines of Mary, Joseph, and Baby Jesus out. Sheri observed that one potato had the shape of a kneeling Mary. Soon she found a taller one for Joseph, and it was easy to find a tiny Baby Jesus. We set up our own nativity scene. My *work* of the moment happened to be peeling potatoes, and this was accomplished, but the greater fulfillment came in seeing Sheri's awareness of the Christmas story expressed in a new way.

I think fulfillment also comes as we build relationships in our work. In any occupation you touch many other lives as you go about your work. A farmer's wife is probably not in contact with others as much as many people, but there are relationships with neighbors and friends and through church and community activities.

A couple of years ago I decided to give up coffee during Lent. But I got so tired of explaining why I wasn't drinking coffee that my Lenten period lasted only three weeks. The point is, it was surprising to me how many people I normally drank coffee with. I think we fail to realize how many contacts we make in our normal activities, and the chances we have to share Christ's love.

One of our big jobs last summer was reshingling the chicken house. This we did as a family project. First, we took off all the old shingles, and nine-year-olds can pull nails as well as anyone. Even John's dad got in on the act, and besides all the help he gave, we enjoyed the time spent with him — probably more than in two or three usual months. Though it was the hottest week of the summer, we took enough swimming breaks to keep it from becoming drudgery. We worked together, ached together, and relaxed together.

During that time a visiting minister, in the course of his sermon, asked our congregation to look at our hands. He said, "Your hands tell a great deal about you." We all saw blisters! Had only Father's hands showed blisters, we'd have hardly noticed, but we were in this together. And, incidentally, the money the girls earned helped them to attend a youth convention.

If work is so fulfilling, should we not drive ourselves harder and harder? My grandpa used to say, "If a little is good, more would be better." This went for such things as eating vegetables, practicing piano, etc. But he found that it's not the way to take medicine!

But does it follow, that the more work, the more fulfillment? A friend of mine complained that her husband was too busy for family vacations, and such things as school activities. "At least," she said, "when he dies everyone will say, 'He sure worked hard.'" And it didn't sound like a compliment. I wonder, when we had temperance lessons, and temperance sermons, did we discuss temperance in work? I think we all agree that work is not the whole of life, but only one segment.

I choose as my text, Psalm 128:1 and 2: "Blessed

is every one that feareth the Lord; that walketh in his ways. For thou shalt eat the labour of thine hands: happy shalt thou be, and it shall be well with thee."

If my "work" is creating a good home climate, a home where there is love and respect for each other, a home where each person can grow and where God is central, yes, I find this work fulfilling. And each day I say a prayer of gratitude for health and for strength to do my work.

Helen Good Brenneman: This book emphasizes there **are as** many ways of being a woman as there are varieties of individuals.

The Author

Born in Harrisonburg, Virginia, Helen Good Brenneman spent her childhood years near Hyattsville, Maryland, a suburb of Washington, D.C. She studied at Eastern Mennonite and Goshen colleges, and worked for four years as a clerk in the U.S. Department of Agriculture. Always interested in writing, Helen longed as a girl to become a newspaper reporter, but later found herself instead writing articles, stories, women's inspirational talks, and devotional books.

Following her marriage to Virgil J. Brenneman in 1947, they served a year in a refugee camp operated by the Mennonite Central Committee in Gronau, Germany, before going to Goshen, Indiana, where her husband studied for the ministry. They served for ten years in two pastorates, at Iowa City, Iowa, and Goshen, Indiana. At the present time Mr. Brenneman is Executive Secretary of the Student Services Committee of the Mennonite Church. The Brennemans are the parents of two sons and two daughters, now in their high school and college years, as well as a foster daughter, Mrs. Jack Birky, of Eugene, Oregon.

Other books by Mrs. Brenneman are *But Not Forsaken, Meditations for the New Mother*, the January section of *Breaking Bread Together*, edited by Elaine Sommers Rich, *Meditations for the Expectant Mother, My Comforters*, and *The House by the Side of the Road.*